T0270648

Absolute Essentials of Strategic Management is an absolute essential for students on a range of business and management courses and practicing managers interested in the seminal and classical works that have shaped strategic management. Its concise and engaging style makes it the ultimate companion for learned colleagues from neighbouring disciplines also curious about this dynamic and all-embracing field of study and application.

Dr Vinh Sum Chau, *Senior Lecturer in Strategy,*
Kent Business School, University of Kent

Absolute Essentials of Strategic Management

Strategy is a foundational aspect of management education, whilst strategic thinking is an essential business skill. This shortform textbook provides the absolute essentials of the field, focusing on how strategy works as a managed process.

The author, an experienced management educator, provides a clear and concise structure that enables readers to understand and excel in the core strategic skills that are essential to contemporary business globally.

This concise and coherent text is a unique alternative to bloated strategic management textbooks and will be welcomed by students and reflective practitioners around the world.

Barry J. Witcher is Emeritus Reader of Strategic Management at the Norwich Business School, University of East Anglia. He has taught at Strathclyde University and Durham University and published in many of the world's leading management journals.

Absolute Essentials of Business and Economics

Textbooks are an extraordinarily useful tool for students and teachers, as is demonstrated by their continued use in the classroom and online. Successful textbooks run into multiple editions, and in endeavouring to keep up with developments in the field, it can be difficult to avoid increasing length and complexity.

This series of shortform textbooks offers a range of books which zero-in on the absolute essentials. In focusing on only the core elements of each sub-discipline, the books provide a useful alternative or supplement to traditional textbooks.

Absolute Essentials of Green Business
Alan Sitkin

Absolute Essentials of Operations Management
Andrew Greasley

Absolute Essentials of Strategic Management
Barry J. Witcher

For more information about this series, please visit: www.routledge.com/ Absolute-Essentials-of-Business-and-Economics/book-series/ABSOLUTE

Absolute Essentials of Strategic Management

Barry J. Witcher

Routledge
Taylor & Francis Group

LONDON AND NEW YORK

First published 2020 by Routledge

2 Park Square, Milton Park, Abingdon, Oxon OX14 4RN

605 Third Avenue, New York, NY 10017

Routledge is an imprint of the Taylor & Francis Group, an informa business

First issud in paperback 2021

British Library Cataloguing-in-Publication Data
A catalogue record for this book is available from the British Library

Library of Congress Cataloging-in-Publication Data
A catalog record for this book has been requested

ISBN: 978-1-138-36537-7 (hbk)
ISBN: 978-1-03-217745-8 (pbk)
DOI: 10.4324/9780429430794

Typeset in Times New Roman
by Apex CoVantage, LLC

Visit the eResources: www.routledge.com/9781138365377

For my wife, Kate

Contents

Introduction

Strategic management is probably the most alive of all the subjects that compose business management. The subject has its fair share of paradigmatic, theoretical, and methodological wars. Issues associated with strategic change and interpretations of what constitutes success and failure are changing all the time. Almost as soon as they are written case studies are out of date and theories fly out of fashion – typically to reappear later in another guise. However, the core ideas which have been developed over time from seminal and classic texts have a long life. The purpose of this *Absolute Essentials of Strategic Management* is to identify these core ideas of strategic management. Be clear about how a particular idea and issue might be appropriate for a particular instance of practice. In so doing, always disentangle your views and your ideas from those of others.

1 Strategic management

Essential summary

Strategic management is the organization's management of its overall long-term purpose. It must not be confused with strategy, which is an organization's overall approach for directing operations to achieve the organization's long-term purpose. An organization's strategy must be used to guide and align the formation of sub-strategies in different parts of the organization.

Strategic planning is the process of planning sequencing activities in terms of responsibilities and resources within a given time-frame to be able to progress an organization's purpose over time.

Strategic change is a step and transformational change that moves an organization to a new and sustainable competitive position and is likely to require changes in existing strategy.

Continuous improvement is organizational learning that sustains and incrementally improves productivity and customer value in daily management, subject to the requirements of an organization's strategy.

Competitive strategy is a business-level strategy designed to sustain a competitive advantage over rivals and potential rivals.

The management of an organization's long-term purpose is called strategic management. A distinction is often made between strategic management and operations. However, the management of operations today must take account of the strategic management of tomorrow. So, strategic management is also about managing an organization in its entirety, including the extent of how operations serve the strategic needs of the organization's strategy. The components of strategic management are shown in Figure 1.1.

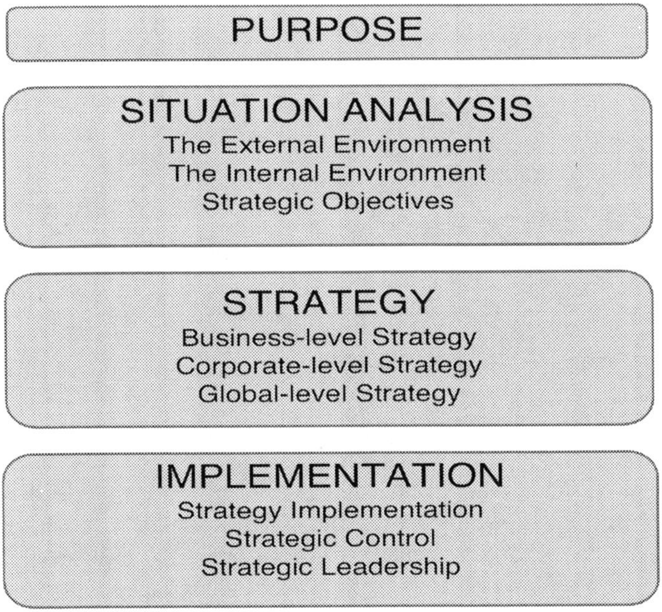

PURPOSE

SITUATION ANALYSIS
The External Environment
The Internal Environment
Strategic Objectives

STRATEGY
Business-level Strategy
Corporate-level Strategy
Global-level Strategy

IMPLEMENTATION
Strategy Implementation
Strategic Control
Strategic Leadership

Figure 1.1 The components of strategic management

Purpose is the basic reason for an organization's long-term existence, and it is the starting point for understanding an organization in its entirety. Purpose is articulated at the top level, and it is communicated from there through purpose statements of vision, mission, and values (see chapter 2). A situation analysis evaluates an organization's current external and internal situations (see chapters 3 and 4); these are used to develop strategic objectives (see chapter 5). The strategy used to achieve strategic objectives is conditioned by the scale and nature of an organization's activities, whether single-business (see chapter 6), multi-business (see chapter 7), or global in orientation (see chapter 8). Implementation includes organizing for managing change (see chapter 9) and strategic control, including feedback and learning through strategic performance management (see chapter 10). In the end, the effectiveness of an organization's strategic management depends on the nature and commitment of top management, its strategic leadership (see chapter 11).

An organization's top management has the ultimate responsibility for managing the components of strategic management. Of course, everybody

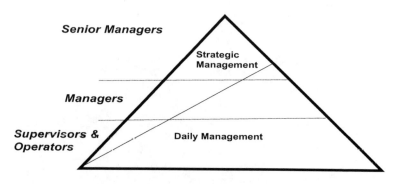

Figure 1.2 Time spent on organizational activities

must be involved to some extent, but it is the senior level that spends most of its time on strategic management (see Figure 1.2). Other levels primarily spend their time on routine management of an operational and functional character. Strategic management therefore must be a top-down directed process, but this has to be done in ways to facilitate bottom-up decision-making and feedback about the feasibility and progress of strategically related work at operational and functional levels.

A top level's strategic objectives and strategy to achieve them must be broken down into departmental strategic objectives and strategies and translated into operational objectives and strategies for daily management. This procedural order is sometimes called a strategy hierarchy, and it must be coordinated to ensure that everyone is working to the organization's purpose.

Strategic planning

Strategic planning is the sequencing of strategic management decisions in advance by an executive or senior management. It is a formal analytic process that provides an organization with a sequenced framework or organizing design to move towards a long-term purpose. At its most simple, strategic planning is equated with POST: Purpose, Objectives, Strategy, and Tactics. At its most complex, strategic planning is known as long-range planning, which examines trends to forecast future events, sometimes far into the future. The high-water mark of long-range planning was during the mid-period of the twentieth century. Forecasting is notoriously difficult: a leading management consultancy, McKinsey & Company, forecast in 1984 that a million mobile phones would be in use by 2000, but the actual number was 741 million.

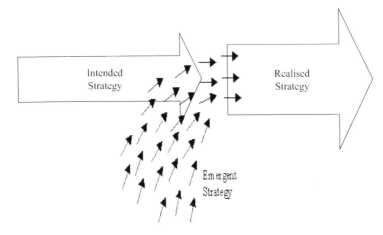

Figure 1.3 Intended strategy into a realized strategy

Strategy scholars began to question the effectiveness of strategic planning. The most well-known critic is Henry Mintzberg (1994), who argued that strategic plans are changed during their implementation as local strategy emerges. In other words, changes to strategy emerge and alter the intended strategy into a different one (see Figure 1.3) (Mintzberg and Waters, 1985). There is an implementation gap between what a top level intends and what lower levels actually achieve. This is not necessarily a bad thing if the changes are incremental and are a logical response to local conditions – a leading strategy researcher, Brian Quinn (1980), called this tendency logical incrementalism.

Mintzberg and Quinn both argue that strategy formulation (the design of objectives and strategy by top management) followed by its implementation (by the rest of the organization) is really an iterative process of strategy formation. Thus, more pragmatic approaches to strategic planning – which require effective organization-wide feedback and review systems – are necessary to enable top management to understand how and why its organization is implementing and making changes to its strategy.

Today, strategic planning is one of the most popular management approaches, but it is typically used as a vehicle for coordinating decentralized strategy-making, which allows lower-level managers to step outside routine pressures to challenge thinking and to redirect their people's time and resources to a common purpose.

Strategic planning is now understood to be a part of strategic management. The Baldrige Excellence Framework defines good practice in terms of a set of management principles (NIST):

1   All tasks must be planned properly.
2   Plans must be implemented so that people are working to these plans.
3   Work must be monitored and progress must be reviewed.
4   Necessary action must be taken to account for any deviation from the plan.
5   Organizations must have structures and management systems to ensure the above work in practice.
6   Everybody must be involved in these structures and systems.

The first four principles correspond to the order of the Deming Cycle – plan, do, check, act (see chapter 4), while the other two cover the necessary provisions of organizational support and a favourable corporate culture. In addition to these management principles, Baldrige specifies that a strategic plan should have

1   A defined strategy,
2   Action plans derived from this strategy,
3   An awareness and recognition of the differences between short- and longer-term plans,
4   An approach for developing strategy based on an organization's external environment and internal strategic resources,
5   An approach for implementing action plans that considers an organization's key processes and performance measures, and
6   An approach for monitoring and evaluating organizational performance in relation to the strategic plan.

While Baldrige does not specify a best way for strategic planning, the list emphasizes the parts that strategic management should have.

Strategic change

Strategic change is transformational change which aims to move an organization to a new position of performance. It works by focusing energy and resources on a few critical success factors or strategic priorities to achieve a new desired state and market position for an organization. So, the direction of change is guided by a strategy that is designed to achieve a vision of a future state. It requires a small number of strategic objectives which senior managers can realistically manage. Given the demands on top management in terms of attention and time, it is important to keep strategy simple and not to get bogged down in too much detail – otherwise you can't see the forest for the trees.

According to Jack Welch (2005), a former chief executive of General Electric, strategy is an approximate course of action that the leadership frequently revisits and redefines according to shifting market conditions. It is an iterative process. This is consistent with Henry Mintzberg's view that strategy is a sense of where you are going – in other words, what direction you and your organization are taking to move your organization forward.

Making substantial strategic change should normally be episodic. It typically happens when threats and opportunities in the external and sometimes in the internal environment call for urgent, radical changes to an organization's existing strategy and business model. Otherwise, overall purpose and the strategy for achieving it should be stable enough to provide a consistent basis for decision-making in an organization as a whole. When conditions are stable, strategic change is actioned through improvement.

Continuous improvement

Change that is continuous is incremental and based on making improvements. These are typically driven by a need to sustain and improve productivity and customer value in daily management. The principle is to stay within a stable business model of an organization's core value-creating areas of the organization. To ensure that an organization continues to be fit for purpose, a number of key performance indicators (KPIs) along with the strategies and targets to achieve them are laid out, typically in the form of a business plan. These are often misunderstood as strategic plans, but to the extent that the KPIs drive best practice, they are really about improving operational effectiveness. While important to sustaining strategy, the substance of daily management may not be very different from that of rivals.

Competitive strategy

Competitive strategy gives an organization an advantage for earning above-average profits within its industry by creating value that is unique compared with that offered by its rivals. This requires a competitive strategy that is sustainable over time. Its role is to integrate and coordinate those organization's activities that make the organization different from rivals in what it does and what it offers. A sustainable competitive difference is not simply doing similar activities better than rivals: it is doing those activities in a way that is hard for rivals to copy at an equivalent cost.

What is strategy?

The terms strategy and strategic management are used interchangeably across teaching courses and textbooks. In fact they are quite different things. The strategy concept is central to strategic management, but like strategic planning, it is only a part of strategic management. Strategy is an approach for directing an organization's operations to ensure its direction and purpose are sustained over time. It acts as a reference framework for all organizational decision-making by clarifying an organization's overall priorities and identifying the main options to progress the direction of activities in line with its purpose.

In thinking about strategy, there are two perspectives that are considered individually but which need to come together, especially for effective competitive strategy. One starts with external market positioning; the other, internal strategic resources (see Figure 1.4).

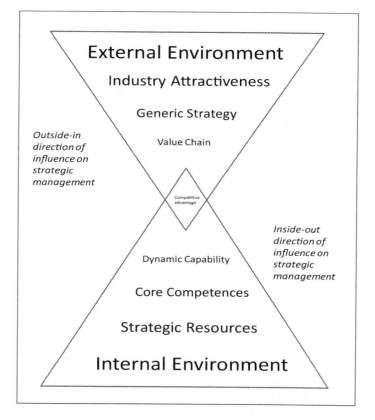

Figure 1.4 Outside-in and inside-out influences on strategy

The most influential work about competitive strategy comes from Michael Porter of the Harvard Business School. His thinking belongs to a well-established industrial organization tradition dating back to the 1960s; this places an importance on the external environment as a determining influence for successful strategy. It reflects outside-in perspectives and is sometimes referred to as market-based thinking. It starts with an analysis of an industry to determine its attractiveness and the choice of a competitive strategy to take advantage of the opportunities. Strategy-related activities are coordinated and optimized through a value chain. The aim is to achieve and sustain a strong competitive position within an organization's industry.

Inside-out perspectives centre on an organization's internal environment and the resource-based view of strategy. Strategic resources are those organizational attributes that combine to give a unique competitive advantage; they are typically core competencies that over time require dynamic capabilities to manage them. The aim is to manage an internal fit of strategic resources to create and sustain a unique competitive difference.

Big-picture strategists are perhaps more likely to take an outside-in view of strategy, compared with hands-on strategists who may be inclined to start with inside-out thinking. It is essential for strategic management to have both. While leaders must have an eye on what is happening in the world, the other eye should have a clear view of day-to-day operations – getting the mix right is absolutely essential:

> You don't want to micromanage every little thing and constrain people in your team. But at the same time, you can't get so preoccupied with a vision or dream . . . It's essential that I get right into the nitty-gritty of how decisions are being executed and make sure things are moving as fast as I want.
>
> (McKinsey & Company, 2012)

The meaning of strategy is much discussed – from the viewpoint of different strategy schools (Mintzberg, Ahlstrand, and Lampel, 1998) to its history dating back to the ancient Greeks (Freeman, 2013). A leading strategy academic, Richard Rumelt (2012), gives a good introduction in distinguishing between good strategy and bad strategy.

References

Freeman, L. (2013), *Strategy: A History*, Oxford: Oxford University Press.
McKinsey & Company. (2012), Leading in the 21st Century: An interview with ICICI's Chanda Kochhar, *McKinsey Quarterly*, mckinseyquarterly.com

Mintzberg, H. (1994), *The Rise and Fall of Strategic Planning*, London: Prentice Hall.
Mintzberg, H., Ahlstrand, B., & Lampel, J. (1998), *Strategy Safari*, London: Prentice Hall.
Mintzberg, H., & Waters, J. A. (1985), Of strategies, deliberate and emergent, *Strategic Management Journal*, 6, 257–272.
National Institute of Science & Technology (NIST), *Baldrige Quality Framework*, https://www.nist.gov/baldrige/publications/baldrige-excellence-framework
Rumelt, R. (2012), *Good Strategy, Bad Strategy*, London: Profile Books.
Quinn, J. B. (1980), *Strategies for Change: Logical Incrementalism*, Homewood, IL: Irwin.
Welch, J. (with Welch S.) (2005), *Winning*, London: HarperCollins.

2 Purpose

Essential summary

Purpose is the reason for the organization and its overall goals.

Vision statement is the organization's statement of its desired future state or ideal.

Mission is the organization's statement of its overriding purpose, such as the value it creates for its stakeholders and other responsibilities.

Values are the organization's statement of its expected collective norms and behaviours and will include its overall core business methodologies and management philosophies.

It is essential for organizations to have a common purpose. There is no sensible strategic management without purpose. This is important if everybody in an organization is to work effectively together. Senior managers spend considerable time clarifying and making purpose meaningful. This is done not only to inspire the organization but also to help employees in an organization to develop their priorities and roles and to understand the priorities and roles of others they work with.

Purpose is the primary and basic reason for an organization's existence, and it is founded on belief. An organization must believe that it serves a useful purpose, and this requires some sort of belief system to make sense of what an organization does since in everyday work much has to go unquestioned. There are three dimensions to how organizations manage themselves as a collective entity – vision, mission, and values. Each offers a different role in strategic management for clarifying organizational purpose (see Figure 2.1).

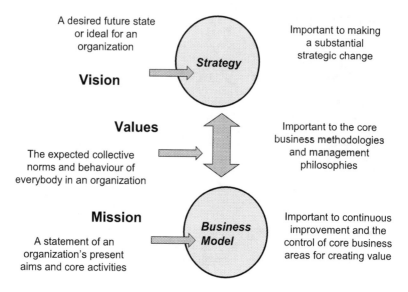

Figure 2.1 The three dimensions of organizational purpose

Vision is a desired future state or ideal for an organization; this requires an organization to make a substantial strategic change. Mission is a statement of an organization's present aims and core activities; these guide an organization's control of its core business areas and continuous improvement for creating customer value. Visionary change and the strategy to achieve it bring change to existing working. Values, the expected collective norms and behaviour of everybody, have a mediating role in terms of how values influence the management of vision and mission together.

Vision statements

Visions are drawn up in document form as a statement of intent. They are typically short and memorably ambitious but not overblown. A vision will provide the basic rationale for change to ensure that the reasons and the broad implications for action are obvious. Its inspirational qualities should excite and motivate enough to encourage people to stretch possibilities and rethink their work. But it also needs to seem realistic – so senior managers need to walk a narrow line between distant ambition and the possibilities of getting there carefully. The development of a vision needs to take into account an organization's situation with regard to both the external and internal environments; this may involve an envisioning process involving the participation of an organization's important stakeholders.

A particular kind of vision statement is a simple 'big idea' – something very different that will change an organization. This can be used as a memorable catchphrase to be easily communicated as a slogan to spur people on to make exceptional efforts. A word of warning is necessary: vision statements should be meaningful statements useful to guide activities in a desired direction and should not be reduced to superficial slogans. It is also essential to understand that they have a different role from that of mission statements.

Mission statements

A mission statement explains why an organization exists. It explains the scope of what an organization does and typically will have a rationale to explain how it adds stakeholder value. The style and the form of statements vary considerably in practice since organizations use them in different ways. For example, a statement can be used for public relations to influence important publics or for marketing to indicate a distinctiveness that stands out against competitors. Care is necessary to ensure that an organization is able to live up to its claims. The statement may claim excellence and quality, but if it fails to deliver these, the organization's reputation will suffer. Platitudes like 'we make your life better' can leave both customers and employees feeling cynical.

The importance of stakeholders to mission is important. Stakeholders are individuals and groups who benefit directly by receiving value from what an organization does and provides. This includes, of course, shareholders and other groups who invest in an organization. They may also include employees, suppliers, and facilitators, such as partners and more broadly society and government. Peter Drucker, widely acknowledged as the father of modern management, in an oft-quoted piece from his classic *The Practice of Management* (1955), puts the customer first:

> If we want to know what a business is we have to start with its purpose. And its purpose must lie outside of the business itself. In fact, it must lie in society since a business enterprise is an organ of society. There is only one valid definition of business purpose: to create a customer.

But a 'customer' can be hard to define for some organizations. In the case of public service organizations, political purpose is important – as well service users and citizens. A major question is about how the wider community can be treated as a customer and how a commercial firm can create significant shared value for society. Corporate social responsibility (CSR) is based on a view that large corporations should fulfil a world citizen role. CSR involves the joint pursuit of profit, good citizenship, and setting a good example by achieving high standards of business morality, especially in relation to practices in the developing world and the environment (Bhattacharya, Sen, and Korschun, 2011).

Values statements

Λ values statement documents the expected collective norms and standards of behaviour for an organization's managers and workforce. It may also be expressed in terms of a set of principles setting out the way that managers and other employees should do and conduct their work. Note that values are different from stakeholder value: values are the standards by which people work, while value is an outcome produced by that work. Values statements should be designed to sustain social capital by emphasizing trust, fairness, support, and honesty – those values upon which most working relationships depend.

In strategic management, values statements have become more important with the rise in growth and power of global organizations. An important reason is a greater requirement to integrate corporate-wide management philosophies and business methodologies across global workforces that differ widely in terms of national cultures. Large organizations have to harmonize cross-functional activity with functional ones, and this needs a general context in which individuals can work consistently in relation to each other to develop and sustain organization-wide values.

An organization's general context for working must be stable over a long period. Jim Collins (2001), in his important book *Good to Great*, argues that the best companies sustain their position by preserving their core values and purpose, while their strategy and operating practices continuously adapt to change. It does not matter what these core values are so much that to be successful companies must have them – it is more important that senior managers are aware of them, can build them explicitly into the organization, and preserve them over time.

An organization's core values constitute its basic strategic understanding, and Collins emphasizes the importance of a culture of self-disciplined people who adhere to a consistent system within which they have the freedom and responsibility to take action. This discipline is felt as much intuitively as it is consciously. It should be communicated through a common organizational culture which is shared by key managers and employees.

Edgar Schein (1985), in his influential book *Organizational Culture and Leadership*, explains organizational culture as the shared basic assumptions and beliefs learned from experience. These operate unconsciously and determine the taken-for-granted perceptions everybody in an organization has of his or her environment. Assumptions and beliefs are forged over time as people learn from dealing with an organization's problems, which become embedded in behaviour that repeatedly proves itself over time. Organizational culture is pervasive and powerful in its influence, so senior managers should be aware and manage its effects for strategic management – or else they are likely to find that culture will manage them.

An established culture is typically organization-specific and because of this it may have given the organization unique ways of working and strategic resources which underpin its competitive advantage. Thus, a new top management should be careful if it wishes to change an organizational culture. It may be more practical to work with a culture than to seek to change it; certainly, with culture it is necessary to build any required changes gradually over time.

References

Bhattacharya, C. B., Sen, S., & Korschun, D. (2011), Leveraging Corporate Social Responsibility: The Stakeholder Route to Business and Social Value, Cambridge: Cambridge University Press.

Collins, J. (2001), *Good to Great: Why Some Companies Make the Leap . . . and Others Don't*, London: HarperCollins.

Drucker, P. F. (1955), *The Practice of Management*, London: Heinemann Butterworth.

Schein, E. H. (1985), *Organizational Culture and Leadership*, London: Jossey-Bass.

3   The external environment

Essential summary

The *external environment* is those conditions external to the organization which influence the organization and its industry, especially those that influence the intensity of competition.

The *PESTEL framework* is a broad but useful mnemonic to group external environmental influences into political, economic, social, technological, environmental, and legal factors.

Structural breaks are fundamental and unpredictable events in the external environment which are likely to require a sudden rethinking about an organization's purpose and strategy.

The *industry life cycle* likens the life of an industry to a living organism that goes through stages of introduction, growth, maturity, and decline; each stage exhibits distinct characteristics that should be considered against the purpose of the organization.

The *five competitive forces* are the primary influences affecting choice of industry and competitive positioning, which affect an organization's competitive advantage and profitability.

Hypercompetition is a dynamic state of constant disequilibrium and competitive change in an industry.

An organization's external environment consists of the conditions outside the organization, including the people and organizations that influence the external changes in the organization's industry, especially those that influence the intensity of competition. External conditions are constantly changing, and organizations need to monitor and review strategy continuously to effectively manage any emerging threats and to be able to exploit advantageous opportunities. Many changes are difficult to identify, and their consequences are often uncertain and even unknowable. The starting point is to monitor and review the background trends to identify and assess opportunities and threats; this drives the strategic management process from the outside in.

The PESTEL framework

The most comprehensive and most used approach for grouping and reviewing macro-environmental trends in strategic management is *PESTEL*, which is a mnemonic for political, economic, social, technological, environment, and legal factors. Changes over time in any of these areas are liable to lead to the transformation of industries. If an organization monitors and audits its external environment it will be better able to respond to trends and respond more quickly to change than its competitors. As the old saying goes – 'The early bird catches the worm.'

While the framework comprises six categories, it is important to use it as an integrated, not compartmentalized view of trends and changes. Strategic management is about seeing and understanding connections and is not concerned with isolated trends but with the management of the BIG picture. Of course, picking out critical details is vital for understanding how change may occur but only in terms of what this suggests for an organization's strategic management. It is important to understand how trends may work together to drive change and innovation. There will be opportunities as well as risks. A periodic PESTEL review challenges strategists to think about long-term trends and raise questions, such as, 'Will our overall strategy give enough flexibility to deal with new forms of competition?'

Political trends

Political factors include trends in not only the actions of local, national, and international governments and agencies but also the thinking and activities of influential groups and individuals. Competition in many areas is shaped by government policies and regulatory decisions. For example, great uncertainty is hanging over global markets because of a possible trade war between the United States and China.

Economic trends

Economic trends include resource use and prices, interest rates, disposal income, economic growth, inflation, and productivity. Since the financial crisis of 2008, the emergent economies of China, India, and some other Asian countries have led the world in rates of economic growth. While globalization has slowed down in the wake of the global financial crisis, it shows every sign of continuing albeit at a slower pace.

Social trends

Social factors include demographic, social and lifestyle trends, group identities and gender roles, national cultures, ethics, morality, and expectations. The post-WWII baby boom in Western countries brought into existence a sizeable and distinct group of consumers who, as they age, will spend more on health and leisure.

Technological trends

Technology includes the impact of new and developing technological change on resources, organizational behaviours, products and services, and operations. The prevalence of smartphones and price scanning applications and the increased use of the Internet are transforming the nature of shopping and the role of information more generally.

Environmental trends

Environmental factors include not only quality of life, sustainability, and recycling of resources but also logistical possibilities and infrastructure. Issues such as world resources, global warming, and pollution caused by plastic packaging and intensive farming are intensifying and will have to be taken into account by most organizations.

Legal trends

Legal factors include laws and regulatory action, standards, border requirements, labour regulations, and so on. This may also include globalization issues dealing with international trade and competition law. National legal frameworks vary considerably, and their consequences for individual industries are profound. One of the most significant trends is the tightening of regulatory accounting standards following large corporate failures – such as Enron, Tyco International, Peregrine Systems, and WorldCom – and the bursting of the dot.com bubble.

The PESTEL process

The PESTEL process should be kept as simple as possible with the big picture always kept central. The use of the approach should follow this set of principles:

1   Someone should be in charge of the process, including meetings and discussions.

2 Before starting, think through the process and be clear what the objectives of the PESTEL analysis are.

3 Keep it simple; do not get bogged down in detail so that the big picture gets lost.

4 Involve a balance of pessimists and optimists; include outsiders with different perspectives and beware of vested interests and group-think.

5 Agree on appropriate sources and check inside the organization first for information.

6 Use visual tools and discussion aids.

7 Identify the most critical factor issues for strategy.

8 Produce a discussion document for wider circulation.

9 Use feedback and follow-up checks on actions and keep all PESTEL participants informed on follow-up to encourage continual dialogue.

10 Decide which issues to monitor on an ongoing basis; link to existing in-house processes for monitoring and reviewing change, especially for planning.

PESTEL is a useful framework to check and determine strategic priorities since managers are encouraged to look beyond their organization and industry and to be less insular. But beware of weaknesses in the method. It can be too easy to scan data and over time slip into lazily ticking boxes. A good PESTEL should go deep enough to consider the root causes behind the trends; things are not always as they appear. The analysis should not merely highlight the obvious; strategists should avoid information overload. Issues should be strategic, not operational, and always relevant to an organization's purpose. There should be a concentration on those factors and issues of most relevance to driving change. Be mindful that ideas are always a question of creativity and judgement – be critically creative.

Black swans and structural breaks

PESTEL analysis is primarily about monitoring and reviewing longer-term trends, but there are also single events that cannot easily be foreseen. These are structural breaks that subvert trends and change existing behavioural patterns. These will require organizations in general to rethink their purpose and overall strategy. Some are so potentially catastrophic that a societal and perhaps a world response are required. The World Health Organization's projected the impact of influenza A/H5N1 pandemic (avian/bird flu) is 7 to 350 million deaths.

David Hume used the discovery of black swans in Australia to illustrate that no matter how many times something can be proved – that swans are always white – it takes only a single event to prove it untrue. This example was developed by Nassim Taleb (2007) in his book *The Black Swan*, in which he wrote about events that cannot be predicted. When they occur, they have a massive impact that takes everyone by surprise. The global financial crisis in 2008 was a good example of a structural break.

Compliance requirements have helped to drive the documentation of strategic risks in organizations. The US Securities and Exchange Commission requires publicly listed companies to document the key business areas and the underlying assumptions that are core to strategic success. This is central to strategic risk management – a systematic and overall approach for managing external events and trends that could seriously harm an organization's effectiveness for achieving its longer-term purpose. It should be a central part of any organization's strategic management.

Strategic risk management should have these key aspects:

1   A statement of an organization's value proposition in relation to business objectives
2   A definition of risks based on the organization's objectives and supporting business strategy
3   A statement on the required corporate culture and behavioural expectations with regard to risk taking
4   A definition of organizational ownership of risk management strategy at organizational levels
5   A description of the management framework or system being employed to deliver the above requirements
6   A definition of the performance criteria employed for reviewing the effectiveness of the risk management framework

While there is no useful way to see when structural breaks and the risks they bring will occur, a PESTEL analysis is likely to raise questions like 'what if?' Downturns in the world economy occur every few years, and there have been four global recessions in the last 50 years. While the timing of a future downturn is uncertain, it is possible to learn something from past events. Some industries, for instance, seem able to weather recessions better than others, such as utilities, telecommunication services, health care, and consumer staples, but these are less likely to grow significantly during an upturn. Industries also have their own periodic cycles.

Industry life cycle

The industry life cycle likens the life of an industry to a living organism: markets expand over time, eventually maturing and finally declining. The life cycle has introduction, growth, maturity, and decline stages (see

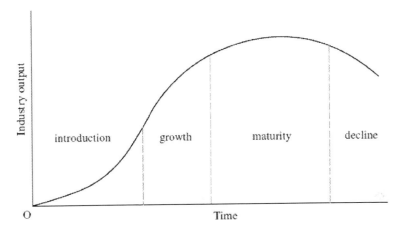

Figure 3.1 Industry life cycle stages

Figure 3.1). The competitive conditions of the industry change as the stages change.

Introduction stage

In the beginning, production is low, costs are high, and demand is very low. There may be a large variety of products and services and diverse organizations. Small entrepreneurial organizations are typically involved, but well-established organizations from other industries may be diversifying and entering a new industry to test the water. An important barrier to entry may be based on knowledge of a developing technology, and large organizations acquire this by taking over small specialist firms. The first to perfect a robust design and applications may be able to capture a significant part of the future market as a first mover. Success is not necessarily based on either best function or lowest cost but rather a robust product supported by a marketing mix that locks in first users, who often buy for reasons of novelty, and early adopters, who are into the personality of the brand.

Growth stage

This is the time when first movers become well established and take dominant positions in their industries. Expansion comes as customers, distributors, and retailers become familiar with the new products and as supplier organizations gain experience and exploit greater economies of scale to offer lower prices. A tipping point is reached at a sales threshold when a band-wagon effect gathers force and the number of competing organizations first rises and then reduces to a handful as a dominant design establishes itself.

Maturity stage

A mature industry is relatively stable, and competition has reduced to a handful of rivals. The term category killer is sometimes used by observers to describe an organization that has been able to eliminate most of the competition for a category of product or service. During the maturity stage, it is no longer possible to maintain individual growth rates without capturing market shares from other rivals. Generally, because of large-scale production advantages, prices are low and rivals compete through distribution and brand loyalty. Economies of scale and branding constitute significant barriers to entry to the industry. If the number of surviving companies is fairly large and similar in size, oligopolistic positions may mean they are well placed to avoid price wars and be able to take advantage of high prices and earn high profits. The maturity stage is also a time when a basic product or service is developed as a range of different but related offers. Each offer is subject to its own product life cycle when the marketing programme is changed to suit the evolving needs of the segment.

Decline stage

The reasons for decline may lie embedded in the general environment and in any of the PESTEL factors. An important reason is a change in technology, although sometimes old technology can rally – a 'sailing ship effect' – when steam ships were introduced, sailing technology actually became more efficient. In modern times the convergence of computing, telecommunications, and media technology has transformed industries, bringing about new life cycles.

Do industry life cycle models work?

An industry life cycle model helps strategists identify the opportunities and threats that characterize different industry environments. Managers need to design their strategy to take account of changing conditions. However, it is often difficult to identify a stage precisely and even more difficult to forecast since there is no universally recognized standard length of life cycles. The strength of the concept lies in its use as a powerful tool for clarifying strategic options as industries and markets develop broadly along trajectories from uncertain beginnings through typically chaotic and intensely competitive growth and afterwards reach more mature and relatively stable states.

The industry life cycle focuses on the characteristics of an industry's stages of development. Nevertheless, it may not be the stages as such but actually how rivals in those stages compete with each other that is important. It is not just the general conditions of an industry and its markets but how rival organizations compete against each other to survive – and the fittest survive:

> Some make the deep-seated error of considering the physical conditions . . . as the most important for its inhabitants; whereas it cannot, I think, be disputed that the nature of the other inhabitants with which each has to compete is generally a far more important element of success.'
>
> (Charles Darwin, 1859)

The five competitive forces

Arguably the most influential contribution to thinking about competitive strategy has come from Michael Porter (1980), who introduced the industry profitability and five competitive forces framework (see Figure 3.2). The central force is the intensity of the rivalry between existing competitors; this is influenced by four others – the threat of new business, the bargaining power

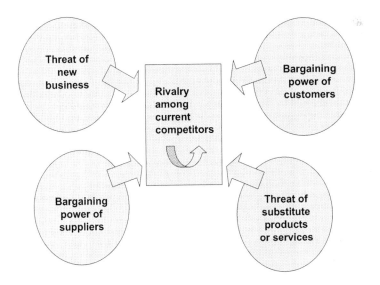

Figure 3.2 The five competitive forces

of customers, the bargaining power of suppliers, and the threat of substitute products and services. The strength of these forces and the way they influence each other determine an industry's profitability and shape its structure.

Porter contrasts the global automotive industry, the international art market, and the regulated health care industry in Europe and observes that, while each is different on the surface, the profitability of each industry is conditioned by the same underlying driving forces of competition. The principle facing the strategist is how an organization can sustain an advantageous position in its industry.

If the competitive forces are intense, an organization is unlikely to earn attractive returns on its investment. If they are weak, above-average returns are possible. Many factors have an influence on short-term profitability, but it is important to realize that the five competitive forces are factors that apply to the longer-term. For example, while the price of food moves up and down depending upon the weather and the cost of fuel for storage and transport, the general and longer-term profitability of supermarkets rests on the bargaining power of the retail chains in relation to their suppliers and customers. The threat of new entrants is low, and the scope for substitutes for groceries is limited.

An individual organization must consider its industry structure as well as its own strategic position within the industry if it is going to defend itself and shape an industry's forces in its favour. The nature of the forces differs by industry, and the strongest force may not be obvious. For example, the threat of new business has been low for supermarkets. Traditionally, the value created for customers of supermarkets lies in their convenience and low costs, and this has critically depended for the customer on the location of the stores. However, Internet shopping now poses uncertainty for longer-term profitability.

The threat of new entrants (new business)

New competition from outside brings additional capacity pressures on existing market shares that influence prices, costs, and investment in an industry. For this reason many existing firms in a threatened industry may hold down profitability to make their industry less attractive to possible entrants. If entry barriers are low and industry profitability is high, new business can enter the industry and drive down prices and raise costs for the existing competitors. The challenge for new entrants is to find ways to overcome the entry barriers without the heavy costs of investment that cancel out the profitability of operating in the industry. There are eight sources of barriers to entry that entrants have to consider and overcome:

1   *Supply-side economies of scale* – incumbents have a cost advantage over incumbents from economies of scale and can sustain lower prices.

2   *Demand-side benefits of scale* – incumbents have a reputation for quality and service that comes from size.
3   *Customer switching costs* – there is a high cost to customers of incumbents in switching to entrants.
4   *Capital requirements* – cost and availability for investment in new areas are likely to be high for entrants.
5   *Incumbency advantages independent of size* – there are advantages stemming from first advantage, such as proprietary technology, access to resources, and locations.
6   *Unequal access to distribution channels* – fewer wholesale and retail channels may mean these are tied up by incumbents.
7   *Restrictive government policy* – competition policy, regulation, and licensing may foreclose entry to entrants from overseas.
8   *Expected retaliation* – the ability and history of incumbents to retaliate when faced with new competition may deter entrants.

The bargaining power of customers

Powerful customers or groups of customers can force suppliers in an industry to lower prices, demand more customized features, and force up service and quality levels. This activity drives down an organization's profitability and shifts the balance of power and value in favour of buyers. Customers have an advantage if the following conditions apply:

1   Customers are few and buy in quantities that are large in relation to the size of suppliers: if the fixed costs of suppliers are high and marginal costs are low, there are likely to be attempts to keep capacity filled through discounting.
2   The industry's products are standardized or undifferentiated: if buyers can find equivalent products elsewhere, suppliers can be played off against each other.
3   Customers have low switching costs in changing suppliers.
4   Customers can produce the product themselves if a supplier is too costly.

Buyers are likely to be sensitive to prices if the cost of the product or service is a significant proportion of its costs and are likely to search for best deals and to negotiate hard. The opposite is true when price forms a low percentage of a buyer's costs. In general, however, price is less important when the quality of the supplied product and its influence on the buyer's own products are vital considerations. The importance of service, especially when quick response and advice are required from the supplier, can be much more important than price. Also, cash-rich and profitable business customers with healthy enterprises may be less sensitive to levels of price. Intermediate customers and customers who are not the end-user of the final product, such as in distribution, are similarly less motivated by price. Producers often attempt to reduce the power of channels through exclusive arrangements with distributors and retailers.

The bargaining power of suppliers

The strength of suppliers will influence the profitability of customer organizations; if this is strong, suppliers can negotiate higher prices to their advantage. This is likely to apply if any of the following conditions apply to an industry's suppliers:

1   Supply is more concentrated than the industry's customers.
2   Suppliers are not dependent upon a single industry for their revenues.
3   Suppliers have customers with high switching costs and close supply chain relations with customers.
4   Suppliers with differentiated products and services are less dependent on individual customers.
5   Suppliers have products and services for which there are no substitutes.
6   Suppliers have a potential to integrate forward and enter a customer's market.

The threat of substitute products and services

Substitutes are nearly always present but are difficult to identify if they appear different in form from an industry's products or services. However, the threat of substitutes influences an industry's profitability because it may enable an industry's customers to go elsewhere. The threat of substitutes is high if it is apparent that alternatives offer an attractive price-performance trade-off to the industry's offer. The customer's switching cost must be low not just in terms of costs but also in terms of convenience and assurance.

Rivalry among existing competitors

This competitive force is influenced by the other four and is the most powerful, depending upon how aggressively rivals are using the other forces to strengthen positions, increase revenue, and save costs. Rivalry is strong when competitors are roughly of equal power and size and are numerous. In this case it is difficult for any organization to win customers without taking them from rivals. Unless the industry has an industry leader which sets the competitive conditions for the industry, competition is likely to be unstable and costly for the industry as a whole.

Slow industry growth, which is a characteristic of mature markets, can stimulate intense competition for market share. This is especially so if exit barriers are high, when organizations are locked into technologies and have specialized resources that are limited in resale value to other industries. Too many suppliers in an industry may lead to chronic excess capacity that is likely to encourage discounting.

Organizations are often present in an industry for a variety of reasons, including non-profit ones, such as the presence of public-service organizations that have social objectives. There may also be organizations that are part of larger groups and are primarily interested in having the experience of the industry's technology and business, which they use to develop products and services in other industries. This may lead to lower profitability in the industry and make it less attractive.

The importance of the five forces

Michael Porter revisited his five force framework in an article published in 2008, in which he summed up its importance:

> Understanding the forces that shape industry competition is the starting point for developing strategy. Every company should already know what the average profitability of its industry is and how it has been changing over time. The five forces reveal why industry profitability is what it is. Only then can a company incorporate industry conditions into strategy.

An organization's competitive strategy can be based on building defences against the five forces or on finding a position in an industry where the forces are weakest. Porter warns that an organization should be careful not to set in motion dynamics that will undermine the attractiveness of the industry in the longer-term. However, for some industries, especially those emerging from new technologies, the short-term may be more important.

Hypercompetition

The short-term is important in conditions of hypercompetition, described by Richard D'Aveni (1994) as a competitive state of constant disequilibrium and change. The concept gained popularity in the early years of the Internet and the rise of the new dot.com enterprises. In emerging and rapidly changing markets competitive advantage is transient rather than sustainable, and organizations typically move on before competitors can react. There is an emphasis on renewing rather than protecting an existing market. A related idea is disruptive innovation, an idea described by Clayton Christensen (1997) as a revolutionary product that replaces existing ways of competing. There are two basic forms: the first acts to create new competition with new markets and customers; the second acts to generate new value for existing customers who are located in a low value-added part of a market, where existing competition is concentrating effort up-market rather than defending low-end segments.

Michael Porter (1999) has noted that new competition generated by e-commerce has encouraged many observers to claim that there can be little advantage in sustaining a competitive strategy over time and that organizations instead should be nimble, quick, and able to learn as change happens. While this may be true, Porter suggests the danger is that this leads organizations to compete only on best practice rather than on competitive difference. In the end, because rivals do similar things and offer similar products and services, customers choose only on prices, and the resulting price competition will eventually undermine industry profitability.

Strategic fit

Strategic fit is matching the opportunities of the external environment with an organization's internal capabilities. The opportunities and threats suggested by PESTEL, the industry life cycle, and the five competitive forces have to be assessed against the strengths and weakness of the organization's internal environment. How good this fit is will be an important determinant of the strategic success of the organization in achieving its purpose.

References

Christensen, C. M. (1997), *The Innovator's Dilemma: When New Technologies Cause Great Firms to Fall*, Boston, MA: Harvard Business School Press.

D'Aveni, R. (1994), *Hypercompetition: Managing the Dynamics of Strategic Manoeuvring*, New York: Free Press.

Darwin, C. (1859), *On the Origins of Species*, London: John Murray.

Porter, M. E. (1980), *Competitive Strategy: Techniques for Analyzing Industries and Competitors*, Boston, MA: Free Press.

Porter, M. E. (1999), A conversation with Michael Porter: A "significant extension" toward operational improvement and positioning, an interview by Richard M. Hodgetts, *Organizational Dynamics*, 28(1), 24–33.

Porter, M. E. (2008), The five competitive forces that shape strategy, *Harvard Business Review*, January, 79–93.

Taleb, N. N. (2007), *The Black Swan: The Impact of the Highly Improbable*, New York: Random House.

4 The internal environment

Essential summary

The *internal environment* comprises of those conditions internal to the organization, including the organization's strategic resources, abilities, and management capabilities.

The *resource-based view of strategy* (RBV) is based on the view that competitive advantage and superior performance are based on the internal management of strategic resources.

The *VRIO framework* – value, rarity, inimitability, and organizational support – is a mnemonic that identifies four key criteria for assessing which capabilities are strategic.

Core competences are organization-specific abilities that an organization's people have which enable them to sustain competitive advantage and superior performance.

Dynamic capabilities allow an organization to renew and re-create its strategic capabilities, including its core competencies, to meet the needs of a changing environment.

Organizational learning is broadly of two kinds – incremental, based on the organization's experience of routine working and existing knowledge, which is called exploitive learning; and innovatory, based on unfamiliar working and new knowledge, which is called exploratory learning.

An organization's internal environment consists of the conditions inside an organization, including its strategic resources, abilities, and management capabilities. An organization's competitive advantage primarily depends upon its managerial and organizational processes. All organizations are different, and this difference can be recognized by management and used to drive the strategic management process from the inside out. As a general point, while being in the right industry matters, it is also necessary to be good at what you do.

The resource-based view of strategy

The resource-based view of strategy (RBV) is a view of strategic management as the management of strategic resources. These are internal strategic assets, such as core competencies and how employees work in ways that are unique to a particular organization; as such they provide a competitive advantage that is difficult for rivals to understand and imitate. Edith Penrose (1959) suggested in her book *The Theory of the Growth of the Firm* that 'resources' should be defined in terms of their value in supporting strategy rather than as narrow economic resources defined by their market value. Strategic resources may have little general market value, but according to the RBV, firm-specific resources matter most to competitive difference.

The VRIO framework

Jay Barney (1997) offers the VRIO framework as a means to identify strategic resources; he suggests that above-average profits are likely if an organization's attributes are

1   Valuable – when they enable an organization to implement strategy that improves its effectiveness and efficiency;
2   Rare – few, if any, competing organizations have these valuable attributes;
3   Inimitable – the attributes are too difficult to emulate because they have a unique history and development, their nature is ambiguous or socially complex; and
4   Organizable – an organization can manage and exploit the competitive potential of the first three.

Strategic resources that meet the VRIO criteria can be enhanced in combinations of different ways – by the recruitment of people with certain aptitudes and knowledge, patents and proprietary technologies, physical assets like buildings and other facilities, location, social and business networks, alliances, and so on. The importance of intangible resources, such as corporate image, brands, and customer service, is also fundamental to establish how people will perceive the difference between organizations and the products and services they offer. Intangibility is quintessentially a holistically sensed quality. All organizations are to some extent unique bundles of attributes, and it is how these are used and managed that determines differences in organizational performance. The key thing is to strategically manage the integration of resources so the intangibility of the whole creates an image that puts the organization apart from its rivals. Central to this is how managers and other employees manage and do their work.

Core competencies

Core competencies are the organization-specific competencies people have which are shared and used in common in ways that give the organization its competitive advantage. They have the following advantages:

1   They are hard for rivals to understand how they work, and they are difficult to copy.
2   They are relevant to a range of markets and industries.
3   They provide a shared understanding of an organization's purpose, and top-down objectives can be better understood and easily implemented.
4   They promote cross-functional working for teams and project management generally.
5   They facilitate a common language of objectives which are managed in a similar way across the organization.
6   They promote a common set of learning-based tools and working principles for solving problems.
7   They facilitate bottom-up management for decision making.

A core competency is not simply an ability to be good or even to excel at a job if rivals are able to copy the competency. Core competencies produce a different way of working and a competitive difference that rivals cannot emulate. An organization's core competencies are characterized as bundles or patterns of skills, knowledge, and supporting resources which give the organization its idiosyncratic pattern of competencies that are core to its strategic purpose. These are typically reinforced and strengthened over time so that they follow a path or trajectory.

The weakness is that once trajectories are formed they become entrenched and are hard to change when the need arises. A strategic lock-in occurs when core competencies are inflexible and difficult to change quickly. The ability of an organization to manage its core competencies over time is referred to in strategic management as a strategic dynamic capability.

Dynamic capabilities

David Teece, Gary Pisano and Amy Shuen (1997), in a seminal journal paper, define a dynamic capability as an organization's ability to integrate, build, and reconfigure core competencies to meet change. A more general definition is an organization's ability to renew and re-create its strategic capabilities (including core competencies) to meet the needs of a changing environment. From the perspective of strategic management this is a senior-level strategic management process, but lower-level capabilities will also be strategic in the sense of their being cross-functional processes, such as product development, alliance and acquisition capabilities, resource allocation, and knowledge transfer routines.

Teece, Pisano, and Shuen identify the Toyota Production System as an example of a dynamic capability. All automakers now have similar lean production systems to that of Toyota, which suggests it is no longer a uniquely distinctive capability and cannot be a strategic resource in that sense. However, dynamic capabilities are often similar across different organizations, and the real competitive differences are in the detail of their application – factors such as timing, cost, and learning effects – which can produce robust differences in performance.

In particular, it is in the way that dynamic capabilities cluster cross-functional activities including management philosophies and business methodologies that makes dynamic capabilities competitively unique. Lean activities including total quality management (TQM), business excellence, benchmarking, and organizational learning are closely intertwined as complementary activities that together add value that exceeds the sum of their parts. An organization's dynamic capability, if it involves a complex integration of these methodologies, is likely to produce a stable pattern of collective activity through which the organization systematically generates and modifies operating routines in pursuit of improvement that really counts strategically.

Lean working

Lean working (or lean production as it is known in manufacturing) is a management system for ensuring any non-value-creating activity is removed. The driving principle is to link the management of an organization's core business processes to strategic objectives to continuously improve customer value. Many assume that lean is an operational tool used only to save waste and costs, but it is much more than this since lean is applied to the organization's critical business or core areas that are important both to a customer value proposition and also competitive strategy. Senior managers identify and specify these areas to give them priority for monitoring and reviewing to ensure the organization remains fit for purpose.

Total quality management (TQM)

TQM is an organization-wide philosophy and set of management principles for improving continually the quality of a product/service to meet customer

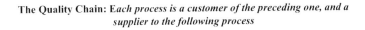

The Quality Chain: *Each process is a customer of the preceding one, and a supplier to the following process*

external customer

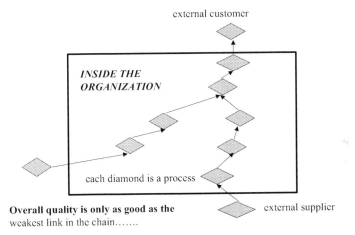

INSIDE THE
ORGANIZATION

each diamond is a process

Overall quality is only as good as the
weakest link in the chain.......

external supplier

Figure 4.1 The quality chain

needs. The 'total' principle is that customer quality is only as good as the weakest link in the quality chain (see Figure 4.1).

Every part of the production and delivery chain must be good enough to give the next work process exactly what it wants for it to produce exactly what is needed by the following process and so on. Discipline is needed throughout the supply chain to ensure that parts and services are delivered exactly when and where needed. The quality chain can be envisaged and applied along the whole supply chain to include external organizations.

If teams have responsibility to control their work to meet their immediate customer's requirements, they are likely to see their work not as a static and standalone process but as a dynamic activity which changes with the needs of the organization's strategy. The guiding principle is that every process is managed according to the Deming (or PDCA) Cycle (Deming, 1986):

1   Plan – what has to be done
2   Do – carry out the work to plan and monitor
3   Check – progress of work and review
4   Act – if required take corrective action or amend plan, the cycle starts over

In a TQM-conditioned environment, PDCA is used for any business process, including strategic management. It forms the basic mechanism for organizational learning. PDCA drives continuous improvement (sometimes called kaizen) in lean working. As a purely operations-based approach, TQM is largely only about taking corrective action to improve a business process. However, when business processes are linked to the achievement of strategic priorities, an external dimension is brought to make TQM strategically sensitive. This happens with kaizen in lean working when organizations use hoshin kanri (policy deployment) to deploy strategic priorities in the daily management of processes.

Business excellence (audit) models

Excellence models are used to audit good management practice in the general core areas of a business or organization; a common name is self-assessment, and the main reason is to identify and deploy good practice and organization-wide learning. Organizations design their own frameworks, but most of these are based on three models: the Malcolm Baldrige National Quality Award, the EFQM Excellence Award, and the Deming Prize. The areas for assessment are similar and cover leadership, people, partnerships and resources, and processes. The components that, according to Baldrige, should be in place for strategic planning are noted in chapter 1.

Benchmarking

Benchmarking is a comparison of an organization's practices with those of other organizations in order to identify ideas for improvement and the adoption of useful practices and (sometimes) to compare relative standards of performance. There are two main types. The first is competitive benchmarking, where the benchmarks are normally expressed as measured reference goals for aggregate performance, such as the output of a production line. The other is process benchmarking, where teams may visit another organization, often in an unrelated industry, to study analogous business processes.

From the resource-based view of strategy, the replication of best practice may be illusive since the managerial practices that are most central to competitive advantage are likely to be specific to an individual organization. It is possible that the more benchmarking organizations do, the more they copy each other and come to resemble one another. Porter (1996), in particular, thinks of benchmarking as operational effectiveness – it will reduce costs, but because every competitor will copy, it will not lead to a distinctive competitive advantage on which long-term success depends.

On the other hand, good practice should be learnt if it is consistent with an organization's purpose. Imitation can improve the way an organization performs. To make strategy work and to improve finding best practices, adapting them, and continuously improving them lead to new ideas about products and services. Learning then becomes the norm, where everyone is searching for a better way.

Organizational learning

Central to the resource-based view and the strategic management of core competencies is organizational learning. Chris Argyris and Donald Schon (1981) distinguish three different kinds: single loop, double loop, and deutero-learning. Single-looped learning involves identifying and correcting errors in existing ways of working: there is a single feedback loop that checks performance against existing plans. The second involves a double feedback loop, which not only connects errors to present plans but also involves questioning the assumptions of the plans and the measures defining effective performance: double loops look beyond the present ways of doing things. Deutero-learning involves monitoring and reviewing how learning is used to manage work, an essential prerequisite for organizational adaptation.

These three types of learning correspond to three different forms of review: single feedback is most associated with routine daily management in operations; double feedback is mostly associated with periodic reviews of strategy; and deutero-learning is important for business audits of how an organization learns and manages its core processes (see chapter 10).

James March (1991), writing from the resource-based view of strategy, makes a distinction between explorative and exploitive learning. Exploration covers unfamiliar sources of knowledge, search, and discovery, while exploitation is concerned with existing knowledge. In other words, explorative learning is the pursuit of new knowledge of things that might come to be known, while exploitive learning is the development of things already known. It is generally thought that an organization should be ambidextrous and use structures and processes that favour explorative learning for major innovation and exploitive learning for incremental improvement.

Some observers suggest that organizations will do better to use exploratory learning if their industry environments are unstable and changeable, while the use of exploitative learning is preferable for stable conditions. For instance, for organizations in mature stages of their industry life cycle, innovation may be stimulated by pressures to reduce costs, improve quality, and increase productivity rather than stimulated by strategic change. William Abernathy (1978) pointed to a productivity dilemma – a possible trade-off between the possible gains in productivity against possible losses in innovative capability. The dynamism of globalization up to the financial crisis of 2008 may have favoured explorative innovation rather than exploitative improvement

approaches. If so, slower growth in developed economies since then may
have swung the pendulum the other way.

References

Abernathy, W. J. (1978), *The Productivity Dilemma: Roadblock to Innovation in the Automobile Industry*, London: Johns Hopkins University Press.

Argyris, C., & Schon, D. (1981), *Organizational Learning*, Reading, MA: Addison-Wesley.

Barney, J. B. (1997), *Gaining and Sustaining Competitive Advantage*, Harlow, England: Addison-Wesley Publishing.

Deming, W. E. (1986), *Out of the Crisis: Quality, Productivity and Competitive Position*, Cambridge: Cambridge University Press.

March, J. G. (1991), Exploration and exploitation in organizational learning, *Organization Science*, 21, 71–87.

Penrose, E. T. (1959), *The Theory of the Growth of the Firm*, Oxford: Basil Blackwell.

Porter, M. E. (1996), What is strategy? *Harvard Business Review*, November-December, 61–78.

Teece, D. C., Pisano, G., & Shuen, A. (1997), Dynamic capabilities and strategic management, *Strategic Management Journal*, 18, 509–533.

5 Objectives

Essential summary

Objectives are strategically desired outcomes that must be managed effectively if the organization is to continue to fulfil its purpose.

The *balanced scorecard* is a documented set of objectives and measures grouped typically into four perspectives.

Critical success factors (CSFs) are the factors that primarily account for an organization's success in achieving its strategic purpose.

Key performance indicators (KPIs) are targets used to monitor progress on strategy-related incremental objectives.

Strategy maps are pictorial representations of the relative order of balanced scorecard perspectives, which are used to illustrate cause and effect.

Strengths, weaknesses, opportunities, threats (SWOT) is a mnemonic framework used to strategically analyze an organization's strengths, weaknesses (concerned with internal factors), opportunities, and threats (arising because of changes in external factors).

An objective is a statement of a specific outcome that is to be achieved. Objectives must be meaningful and clear to the people who use them and linked to realistic measures of progress so that those managing the objectives will know in enough time if it necessary to intervene and make appropriate changes. Objectives are the basis of a common language for understanding the context of work and identifying the inevitable knock-on effects of change. Of course, this requires common ways of working that are based on dialogue and consensus to facilitate the development and management of objectives in ways that are transparent and can be understood by all. This makes work easier.

To establish clarity in objectives, conventional objectives should be SMART:

1   Specific
2   Measurable
3   Action-oriented (and agreed upon)
4   Realistic
5   Time-bound

Strategic objectives can be open, general, and intangible; they can also be long term and ambitious – perhaps to an extent that seems unrealistic. This happens when an objective is used as a spur to creative thinking about having to do things differently and to encourage a diversity of solutions for open-ended problems.

Gary Hamel and C. K. Prahalad (1989) write about the simplicity of strategic intent and the use of long-term visionary objectives, such as a simple statement – for example, Komatsu's declared intent to 'encircle Caterpillar'. The aim of such statements is to create an organization-wide obsession that was out of all proportion to an organization's resources and capabilities. This type of objective is an open one, and no one knows what the longer term will look like, but the direction it suggests must be translated into annual business plans to provide operational objectives that are implemented as SMART short-term objectives.

It was Nobel Prize winner Herbert Simon (1947) who first wrote that organizational goals should be set by senior management and then broken down into sub-goals for use at each level of the organization. In this way each lower-order goal becomes a means to a higher-order goal. In this sense there is a hierarchy of objectives (which is analogous to the strategy hierarchy). An organization's overall objectives, such as corporate objectives, are translated and used to deploy lower-level subobjectives. At operational levels objectives are often referred to as targets, and corporate objectives are sometimes called goals. In fact, there is no clear consensus about the use of such terms – goals, targets, aims, and objectives are often used interchangeably. In understanding their meaning, it is important you should carefully note how the particular context in which they are being used defines what they exactly mean.

The general management of objectives

The woes that beset objective management are many, and some of these are summarized as follows. Objectives must not be

1   too many – or subobjectives mushroom out of control;
2   meaningless – to motivate they must seem relevant;

3 useless – must be able to manage, review, and learn from them;
4 old – must be relevant for change;
5 myopic – must be far-seeing and linked to the bigger picture;
6 insular – should not be selfish and easy to do, to the detriment of others;
7 inconsistent – all objectives must work synergistically;
8 pets – should not be favourites of vested interests, to the detriment the bigger picture;
9 non-agreed – all affected parties should be consulted;
10 complex – must be kept simple to be understandable.

Senior levels should strategically manage how objectives are used across their organizations, in particular to ensure that objectives have active owners who take resistibility for progress. Realism and practicality are important. Objectives should clarify what should be achieved. Of course, it has to be recognized they are often subjective and rely on personal judgement. While objectives need to be essential and stable, it must be recognized that as subobjectives and plans progress, it may be necessary to amend or adapt the nature of a strategic objective. Changes in strategic objectives are likely to affect many people, so changes in them should be made rarely, and where possible new options investigated to find an alternative means to achieve the objective. As a working principle, higher-level objectives should be managed by senior managers in ways that keep overall strategy relatively stable over time.

There are no hard and fast prescriptions for setting objectives, but their management must be flexible and based upon an open understanding of an organization's current way of doing things. In other words, how things are done now is the starting point for doing things differently. It is important to manage objectives actively so that different things can be attempted as necessary to achieve a desired result.

Objectives and strategic management

For strategic management, purpose must be translated into a set of primary objectives called strategic objectives. These are used as indicators and measures of progress to guide an organization's long-term purpose. They cover the core areas of an organization and are used to develop the short-term priorities for the implementation and execution of strategy. There is a tendency for managers to react more positively to short-term rather than longer-term objectives. In Peter Drucker's (1955) powerful words,

> There are few things that distinguish competent from incompetent management quite as sharply as the performance in balancing objectives [to] obtain balanced efforts, the objectives of all managers on all levels

and in all areas should be keyed to both short-range and long-range considerations . . . Anything else is short-sighted and impractical.

Critical success factors (CSFs) and key performance indicators (KPIs)

The importance of balance is reflected in the difference between critical success factors (CSFs) and key performance indicators (KPIs), where the former refers to those factors that primarily account for an organization's long-term success and the latter to target measures for achieving outcomes in key operational areas. In modern management the CSF concept is often used to mean those core business processes that must be healthy enough to achieve an organization's purpose; for instance, they might refer to those management areas specified in business excellence models or the core processes identified in lean working for sustaining value (chapter 4).

CSFs are often confused with KPIs, but KPIs should be measures that link daily activities to an organization's CSFs. In other words, while CSF are long term and linked to overall strategy, KPIs are strategically related targets in short-term management. The difference is important to the distinction drawn between strategic objectives and measures in the balanced scorecard.

The balanced scorecard

A balanced scorecard is a documented set of objectives and measures expressed from the point of view of four key areas of organizational concern called perspectives. Robert Kaplan and David Norton introduced the concept in a *Harvard Business Review* article in 1992. It has been widely adopted. Its role is to help organizations take a wide-ranging view of four types of strategically important objectives and their measures: financial, customer, internal processes, and learning and growth. The key essential about the scorecard is that each objective has to have its own measures – true to the old adage that what gets measured gets done. Objectives are typically based on CSFs and the necessity of achieving a strategic vision. The measures associated with them take the form of KPIs, or targets, which indicate timelines along the way to achieving the objectives.

No singe perspective takes priority; the idea is that the perspectives and objectives are to be understood as an integrated set. The total number of objectives must be kept to a bare minimum; otherwise, the scorecard gets too complex. No more than a half-dozen in total is about right. The choice of perspectives is sometimes changed or new ones adapted, such as an addition of a CSR objective to reflect an organization's concern with societal issues. Generally however, the original four perspectives have stood the test of time. The exact choice of objectives and measures varies, but an example of objectives and measures is suggested in Figure 5.1.

The original Kaplan and Norton (1992) article used different names for the internal business processes and the learning and growth perspectives. They were originally called the 'internal business' and the 'innovation and learning' perspectives, and the scorecard was originally considered only a general performance management tool. Within a few years, however, Kaplan and Norton (1996) had proposed a *strategic* balanced scorecard – a strategic management system for the achievement of a vision – and the perspectives

---

Financial Perspective
Objective: To maximise financial returns to the owners of an organization's capital
Measured by:
  •Return on capital employed
  •Payments (e.g. dividends) to owners
  •Cash flow

Customer Perspective
Objective: To sustain customer relationships
Measured by:
  •Customer satisfaction & delight index
  •Repeat purchase patterns
  •Brand awareness in target segments

Internal Processes Perspective
Objective: To create and maximise value in the customer-vendor relationship
Measured by:
  •Value stream analysis (to minimise non-value creation activities) index
  •Value chain activities (coordination, optimisation activities) index
  •Continuous improvement (innovation, change) index

Learning & Growth Perspective
Objective: To motivate people & develop competences
Measured by:
  •Recruitment & retention rate
  •Skills & training index
  •Employee conditions & satisfaction index

Figure 5.1 An example of objectives and measures

were given their present names to reflect the importance of the management of core business processes, core competencies, and learning. This difference is important because in practice some organizations use the scorecard as a performance measurement tool, while others follow the strategic approach.

A performance measurement scorecard can use a higher number of objectives than a strategic one. These scorecards are typically based on existing business models and missions. Strategic scorecards are based on longer-term vision and as such should be kept as simple as possible to give direction to the four perspectives. A typical issue stems from confusion about which objectives are strategic and which are operational. Operational measures are adequate for a performance measurement but should not be used for strategic objectives, unless it is clear how they relate making strategic changes.

Strategy maps

In managing a strategic balanced scorecard, possible strategic causes-and-effects should be worked out to develop objectives and measures and to review their progress over time. Kaplan and Norton (1996) introduced the idea of a strategy map as a reference framework to help management reflect and explore possible cause-and-effect relationships and how they stand in relation to current issues. Thus, a strategy map is a methodology to support and examine the scorecard and to evaluate the basic assumptions for choosing objectives and measures. The idea is to think strategically to explore any possible connections and evaluate them as an interrelated whole.

There is no prescriptive form for a strategy map and directional links between perspectives and objectives must be drawn out according to how managers see the key contributions that enable the organization to reach its vision. The principle stands that no perspective is regarded to the detriment of the others. However, the direction of thinking about cause-and-effect influences flows first from learning and growth (the required learning skills for progressing strategy), next through the internal process perspective (those core processes for vision), next to customers (the value to the beneficiaries), and finally to the financial perspective (provision of revenue, investment). Kaplan and Norton argue against an exact and deterministic-based organizational understanding of objectives and their measures; instead they stress the importance of organizational alignment and communication.

Managing the balanced scorecard

Kaplan and Norton propose a strategic management process involving the balanced scorecard. This is in four parts and starts with senior-level agreement on the appropriate strategic objectives and measures to achieve the organization's vision. The scorecard is then communicated to the rest of the organization so that incentives and rewards are aligned to the objectives and measures. The scorecard is then used as a basis for deciding strategic initiatives, such as projects. The final part is the provision of feedback to enable senior managers to evaluate and learn how the objectives and measures are working and to test the assumptions against the CSFs. It is important that a senior manager's team take full charge of managing the scorecard: the chief executive takes responsibility for the whole process, while each of the four parts of the management process is the responsibility of an individual executive.

In general, organizations are bad at organizing an effective capability for organizational learning at the senior management level. Most managers do not have a procedure to receive feedback about their strategy in a way that enables them to examine the assumptions on which their objectives and measures are based. The scorecard and its accompanying strategy map should give a greater capacity for strategic learning, which, Kaplan and Norton argue, is a cornerstone of a strategic management system. They suggest that a formal administrative function could be used to support the management of the scorecard, such as a strategy office to manage implementation. A corporate-level strategic scorecard may be translated into scorecards for different parts of an organization. Subsidiary scorecards may be developed at operational levels when the corporate objectives and measures are adapted in the light of local circumstances. Also, the designs of scorecards can vary from organization to organization (Witcher and Chau, 2008).

Strengths, weaknesses, opportunities, threats (SWOT)

In developing a strategy to achieve strategic objectives, it is essential that an organization take account of the opportunities and threats present in the external environment and the strengths and weaknesses in its internal environment (Figure 5.2). An analysis must start with the overall purpose of the organization and how this translates into strategic objectives. It should also take stock of the present assumptions and management of that purpose.

SWOT is used as an integrative framework to consider an organization's strengths, weaknesses, opportunities, and threats. It can be used as a quick and simple method or more deeply as a detailed and comprehensive organizing framework. However, the components of analysis must be based on the determination of strategic objectives – the reason for a strategic SWOT. How a balanced scorecard fits into a SWOT scheme is shown in Figure 5.3.

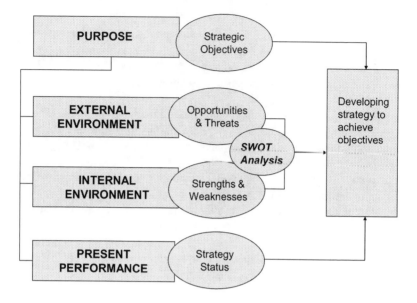

Figure 5.2 SWOT analysis and its place in developing strategy

SWOT ANALYSIS

Financial Performance	Financial Objectives & Measures	OPPORTUNITIES THREATS
		·PESTEL factors
		·Industry profitability &
Environmental & Competitive Situation	Customer Objectives & Measures	*competitive forces*
		·Changes in industry groups
		·Market life cycle
Core Capabilities	Internal process Objectives & Measures	STRENGTHS WEAKNESSES
		·Value creation process
		management
Core Competences	Learning & Growth Objectives & Measures	*·Price & quality*
		·People skills & values
		·Location

BALANCED SCORECARD

Figure 5.3 SWOT and the balanced scorecard

A strategic SWOT is made of the following:

1   Strengths are attributes of the organization that are helpful to achieving the strategic objectives.
2   Weaknesses are attributes that are unhelpful or require attention to make them helpful to achieve the strategic objectives.
3   Opportunities are external influences that are helpful for achieving the strategic objectives.
4   Threats are influences that could harm or prevent the achievement of strategic objectives.

The opportunities and threats relate to the strategic objectives of the financial and customer perspectives of the balanced scorecard, where the outside-in influences of the external environment are important. The strengths and weaknesses relate to the strategic objectives of the internal processes and learning and growth perspectives, where the inside-out influences of the internal environment are considered.

The SWOT analysis process is driven by four basic questions:

•   How can each strength be used and developed to advance the strategic objectives?
•   How can each weakness be improved and converted into a strength?
•   How is it possible to exploit and benefit from each opportunity?
•   How can each threat be addressed and possibly converted into an opportunity?

SWOT is a simple but much-abused idea. It should not be a simple list of bullet points of equally weighted factors, since prioritization is necessary to determine which strengths, for example, matter more than others. For strategic objectives, SWOT analysis should be centred on the CSFs for achieving an organization's purpose. It is therefore helpful if it is carried out alongside the use of a strategy map, which can be used to identify the primary cause-and-effect relationships and will help the participants to identify and sort out the most important SWOT factors. In carrying out a SWOT analysis, in general, the following principles should be observed:

1   Be as realistic as possible.
2   Distinguish where the organization is now and where it wants to be in the future.
3   Be as specific as possible to avoid ambiguity and confusion.
4   Keep the SWOT short and comprehensible.
5   Question several times to clarify the logic of why a factor is relevant.

The composition and number of participants are important. As a team they should be representative of the core business areas and able to see the overall and complete picture. The ideal number for an open discussion is eight. Using a balance scorecard approach for SWOT analysis helps to bring a balance of external and internal considerations to the process. Otherwise, there is a tendency to favour either exploratory or exploitative sources of information depending upon the focus and location of the SWOT team in the organization.

For example, strategy making in the periphery of an organization may be more externally oriented than is the case at the centre, which could be more internally focused. Decision-making that is closer to markets may involve more exploratory learning activities, such as scanning and scenarios. Decision-making at the centre of an organization may involve more exploitative forms of learning, such as monitoring and forecasting. The aim should be to strike an overall balance. The essential point, however, is that the objective of a strategic SWOT must be clear at its start if it is to be a useful activity for strategic management.

References

Drucker, P. F. (1955), *The Practice of Management*, London: Heinemann Butterworth.

Hamel, G., & Prahalad, C. K. (1989), Strategic intent, *Harvard Business Review*, May-June, 63–76.

Kaplan, R. S., & Norton, D. P. (1992), The balanced scorecard: Measures that drive performance, *Harvard Business Review*, January-February, 71–79.

Kaplan, R. S., & Norton, D. P. (1996), *The Balanced Scorecard: Translating Strategy into Action*, Boston, MA: Harvard Business School Press.

Simon, H. (1947), *Administrative Behaviour: A Study of Decision-Making Processes in Administrative Organizations*, New York: Free Press.

Witcher, B. J., & Chau, V. S. (2008), Contrasting uses of the balanced scorecards: Case studies at two UK companies, *Strategic Change*, 17, 101–114.

6　Business-level strategy

Essential summary

Business-level strategy is an organization's fundamental approach for enabling a single business to sustain a competitive advantage within a given industry.

A competing single business organization should choose only one generic strategy.

Cost-leadership generic strategy is a single business strategy based on being the lowest-cost organization in an industry.

Differentiation industry-wide generic strategy is a single business strategy based on a uniqueness that offers value for customers and returns that more than offset the costs of differentiation.

Cost focus and *differentiation focus generic strategy* are single business strategies that apply to a particular part of an industry, such as a market segment or niche, where the business concerned is able to design a strategy that more closely meets the needs of customers than could be achieved by rivals.

A *value chain* is an organizational framework for disaggregating and showing an organization's strategically relevant activities, which is used to help understand and manage the behaviour of costs and the existing and potential sources of differentiation.

Business models are conceptualizations of an organization's critical areas or processes for the creation of the organization's unique value for its customers.

A business-level strategy is an organization's fundamental approach for enabling a single business to sustain and develop its overall purpose. Typically, the strategy aims to sustain a competitive advantage within a given industry.

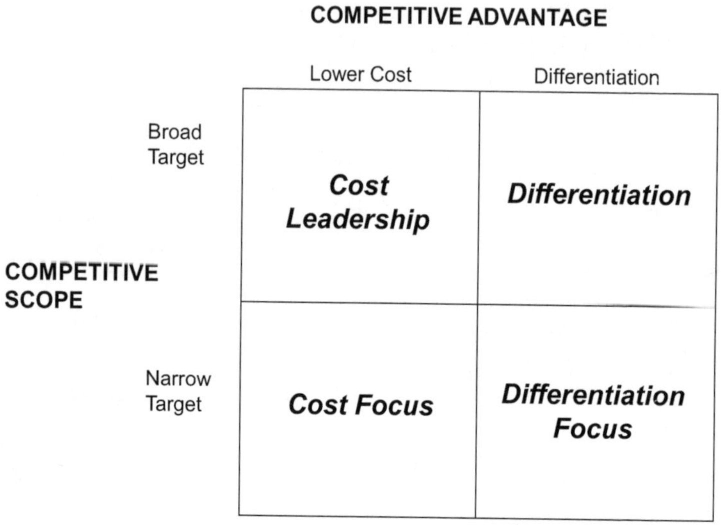

COMPETITIVE ADVANTAGE

	Lower Cost	Differentiation
Broad Target	*Cost Leadership*	*Differentiation*
Narrow Target	*Cost Focus*	*Differentiation Focus*

COMPETITIVE SCOPE

Figure 6.1 Four generic strategies

Strategic management aims to provide a strong long-term competitive position that over time will benefit an organization's stakeholders more lastingly than short-term profitability. It is likely that an external environment will be subject to sudden shocks as well as continuous change, so it is necessary to ensure that strategic priorities are constant and consistent so that the organization as a whole is clear about purpose and can adjust to change accordingly.

There are four broad kinds of competitive strategy based on competitive advantage and competitive scope (see Figure 6.1). Michael Porter (1980) refers to these as generic strategies: when an organization targets a whole industry a strategy is either a cost leadership generic strategy or an industry-wide differentiation generic strategy. When an organization targets a part of an industry, such as a market segment, generic strategy is focused on either cost or differentiation. The detail of a strategy will depend on an organization's purpose and its industry; however, to be competitively effective it must conform to one of the four generic types.

Cost-leadership generic strategy

A cost-leadership generic strategy has lower costs per unit produced than competitors and any potential rivals can achieve in the industry. The term 'leadership' is important since this requires an organization to be *the* cost leader and not just one of several organizations competing on costs. If an organization has a larger share of its industry's markets than its rivals, it can achieve relatively greater economies of scale and scope. Economies of scale are obtained through cost savings that occur when higher volumes allow unit costs to be reduced. Economies of scope involve cost savings that are available as a result of separate products sharing the same facilities.

The advantages of scale and scope are associated with the experience curve effect, an idea introduced by the founder of the Boston Consulting Group, Bruce Henderson (1974). He argued that when the accumulated production of an organization doubles over time, unit costs when adjusted for inflation have a potential to fall by 20–30 per cent. This is the result not just of scale but of a combined effect of learning, specialization, investment, and scale. The more an organization does, the lower the unit cost of doing it will be. When cumulative volume doubles, the extra costs, including those in administration, marketing, distribution, and manufacturing, fall by a constant and predictable percentage.

The experience curve idea has encouraged organizations to try to gain a large market share quickly by investing heavily and aggressively downpricing products and services; the high initial costs can be recovered in the longer term once the organization has become the market leader. Organizations should certainly seek to learn and improve continuously before their competitors do so, but it is difficult to identify an experience curve effect in many industries as its exact nature is often difficult to understand.

The sources of cost advantage are varied and include such things as proprietary knowledge and technology, preferential access to industry distribution channels and sources of supply, and effective cost management. Low-cost leaders often sell a standard or no-frills product and/or service. They place considerable emphasis on taking advantage of scale but are also likely to take advantage of any other opportunities to lower costs.

A low-cost leader does not necessarily have to lower its prices below those of its rivals. It may do this to win more customers and to reap more economies of scale, but if its costs are lower than the industry's average, all it has to do to earn above-average returns is to command prices at or near the industry average. Price competition can be dangerous if it sparks a long price war and discounting eats into profits, but if the leader has a large share of the industry's market it can usually outstay a war that lasts over the shorter term, and lower prices are likely to increase its market share.

Differentiation industry-wide generic strategy

A differentiation industry-wide generic strategy offers unique value for an industry's customers in a way that more than offsets the costs of differentiation, which enables an organization to earn above-average profits for the industry. This may involve a capacity to be able to offer product and service attributes that are offered differently and are different from those of other participants in the industry, such as special qualities; delivery and reliability features; corporate and brand images; advanced technological, service, and support arrangements, and so on.

The organization concerned will seek to reduce its costs but only in a way that does not affect the sources of differentiation and the value it creates. The 'industry-wide' position is important since it involves coverage of the whole industry and its markets. Unlike cost-leadership, there can be more than one successful industry-wide differentiation competitive position in an industry. This happens when there are significantly different and distinctive customer groups that value product and service attributes in contrasting ways.

The development of an industry's markets over time tends to favour differentiation, especially if the industry is associated with consumers with preferences that change frequently and who are affluent. In general, as consumers become more affluent, lower prices may be considered secondary to quality and branding.

Cost focus and differentiation focus generic strategy

A focus generic strategy is based narrowly on a particular part of an industry, such as a market segment or niche, where an organization can design its strategy to meet the needs of customers more closely than its competitors. A focuser does not have an overall industry competitive advantage, but it is able to achieve one in its target segment based on a low-cost base or differentiation. Both these strategies depend on the perception that a target segment is different from others in the industry.

The implication of a focus generic strategy is that more broadly-targeted competitors cannot deliver a comparable value to the focuser's target customers. This may be because they are unable to meet the more specialized needs of a segment or are likely bearing a relatively high cost in serving a segment; both conditions mean that returns in the segment are likely to compare unfavourably with those of a focused competitor. There is normally room for a number of focus strategies within an industry if the focusers choose different target segments.

Generic strategies are mutually exclusive

The essential thing about the four generic strategies is that an organization must choose one only in its industry. An organization that chooses a generic strategy that is a combination of cost and differentiation is called a straddler when it resembles a 'Jack of all trades, master of none'. Being all things to all people is a recipe for strategic mediocrity and below-average performance because, in the view of Michael Porter, an organization will have no competitive advantage at all. Different generic strategies have different resource needs, and divided attention to different kinds of strategies leads to costly trade-offs between different kinds of resources that eat into profitability. Organizations should concentrate on providing value that its rivals in the industry cannot match.

The value chain

A value chain is an organizational framework for disaggregating and showing an organization's strategically relevant activities in order to understand the behaviour of costs and the existing and potential sources of differentiation. The role of a value chain is to identify those strategy relevant activities in the core areas of the organization to assess how they interact together to sustain a chosen strategy. An organization sustains its competitive advantage by performing these strategically important activities more cheaply or better than its competitors.

Value is represented by the amount customers are willing to pay for an organization's products and services. Porter (1985) stresses the importance of activities in adding value, rather than functions, such as departments. Value is shown in the value chain as a margin, which is gross revenue (the aggregated value created for customers) minus costs – or the net margin received by the producer as gross profit (see Figure 6.2). The value-creating activities are shown broadly as primary and support activities.

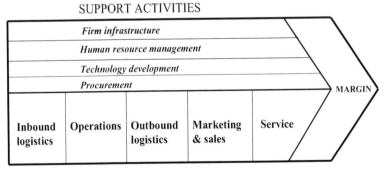

Figure 6.2 The value chain

Primary activities add value through the transformation of resources into products and services through the following stages:

1   inbound logistics: activities bringing in inputs
2   operations: activities turning inputs into outputs
3   outbound logistics: activities getting finished products to customers
4   marketing and sales: activities enabling customers to buy and receive products
5   service: activities maintaining and enhancing value

Conventionally, these are associated with the line functions of a business. However, a value chain is concerned only with those attributes and activities that are strategically relevant and how these interact and can be integrated as a whole system – not in isolation from the perspective of any one functional part of the organization. Support activities add value by facilitating and assisting the primary activities. Conventionally, support activities are typically staff functions and the responsibility of a dedicated department, although they are normally cross-functional in orientation. The figure shows a simplified picture of four functions, but it is possible to have more, such as quality management. The four shown have the following activities associated with them:

1   firm infrastructure: activities such as planning, legal affairs, and finance and accounting, which support the general management of the primary activities
2   human resource management: activities that support the employment and development of people
3   technology development: activities providing expertise and technology, including research and development, which support the production and delivery process
4   procurement: activities to support buying

Senior managers must look for strategic linkages to help them coordinate and optimize resources that promote and sustain competitive advantage. The way of managing an activity in one area of an organization is likely to have spillover and trade-off effects for other areas; for example, lowering costs in one department may be suboptimal if it works to raise costs elsewhere. Coordination is necessary to promote common ways of working in line with the needs of the competitive strategy. A distinctive customer relationship management approach requires attention to every part of those activities that influence the customer experience.

A value chain for cost leadership is shown in Figure 6.3. This is an example for a general insurance company that offers low-price policies and

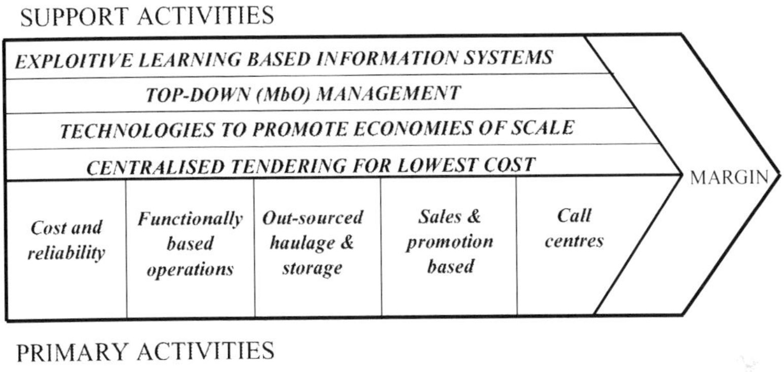

SUPPORT ACTIVITIES

Figure 6.3 Cost leadership

SUPPORT ACTIVITIES

PRIMARY ACTIVITIES

Figure 6.4 Differentiation

aims to achieve economies of scale through taking a large market share. Its internal organization is formally organized and geared up for productivity and efficiency. The value chain tasks are to coordinate and optimize costs subject to continuous improvement. The value chain in Figure 6.4 is an electronics engineering company that supplies office equipment to industrial customers. It offers relatively high prices in its industry but with a good and responsive maintenance service. Its organizational culture is collegial and informal, and there is a strong tradition of innovation. It takes a relatively large market share, which is based on providing its business clients with a customized service. The value chain tasks are to coordinate and optimize the effectiveness of activities that support a customized service that is superior to other industry participants.

Generic strategy and the resource-based view

The rise of Japanese competition during the last quarter of the twentieth century seemed to call into question the exclusivity of choosing only one generic strategy, as Japanese organizations offered differentiation while simultaneously achieving lower costs than those of their Western rivals. They did this largely through superior organizational capabilities, such as lean production and associated business methodologies and philosophies, including business process and lean management (see chapter 4). They seemed to follow a hybrid, or a best-cost differentiation, generic strategy (see Figure 6.5). A best-cost differentiation strategy aims to offer superior value to customers by meeting their expectations on key product and service attributes while also exceeding their expectations on price.

Best-cost differentiation generic strategy fits well into the resource-based view of strategy. The resource-based view has been contrasted in opposition to Porter's ideas about generic strategy. His defence is to explain Japanese strategy as operational effectiveness, not real strategy. This being so, it is still possible to use the value chain concept for the management of a best-cost differentiation generic strategy. In Figure 6.6 an example is given for an automobile company.

While it aims to minimize its costs through economies of scale, lean production and just-in-time management facilitate a demand-pull rather

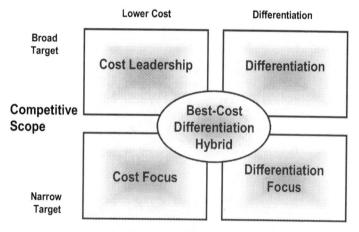

Figure 6.5 Best-cost differentiation

SUPPORT ACTIVITIES

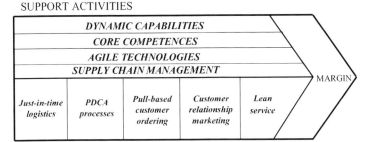

PRIMARY ACTIVITIES

Figure 6.6 Best-cost differentiation

than a supply-push approach for creating value. Senior managers use top-down strategic priorities that encourage bottom-up operational strategies that are designed to achieve both productivity improvements and continuous improvement in customer value. The value chain tasks, following the principles of lean working, are to coordinate and optimize activities that continuously improve value for customers. The value chain for a best-cost differentiation generic strategy is concerned with strategic resources that support the primary activities, as shown in Figure 6.6.

Extending the value chain into the supply chain

The value chain concept can be extended beyond the boundaries of an organization to include those strategic related activities in distribution and the supply chain. This can be envisaged as a series of linked value chains across relevant distributors and suppliers. The idea is that suppliers – particularly first-tier suppliers that supply inputs that are crucial to an industrial customer's creation of value – should manage their activities in ways that are consistent with the business strategy of their customers. Synergies are sought between an industrial customer's core competencies and those of upstream suppliers and between its downstream distributors and customers. The greater the possibilities for an organization to manage a sequence of processes both internal and external, the more difficult it is for rivals to emulate its activities. However, the extent to which a business strategy and value chains of independent suppliers can be influenced to support an industrial customer is problematic. For small and specialized suppliers there is always a fear of losing bargaining power when a large part of their production is tailored towards the needs of a big customer.

Business models

A business model is a description of an organization's core business areas (and CSFs) and processes for achieving the overall purpose of the organization, especially how the organization captures value (Chesbrough and Rosenbloom, 2002). A model may illustrate how the organization delivers a unique customer proposition and a competitive difference. Business models and strategy are often used interchangeably, but a business model is typically stable and based on an established mission. A strategy that aims to bring about a radical change, such as one to move the organization to a new visionary position (as for the strategic balanced scorecard), can work to change the underlying business model. In other words, a business model is based on mission, while a change strategy is based on changing that model.

Nevertheless, a generic competitive strategy should be stable over time – Porter suggests decades; otherwise, the strategy will lack the consistency to enable an organization to continuously improve and sustain its competitive position in an industry over time. The trajectory of strategic resources and development of core competencies also take time to develop. In this light, a strategy designed to effect strategic change is best considered as a strategic programme to further sustain purpose that would not otherwise be achieved given an existing generic strategy and business model.

A strategy imposes discipline, be it in the form of a business model or a strategy to manage change. A successful strategy is as much about not doing things that dilute effort and impact as it is about doing things that focus effort and impact. A clear strategy requires understanding by everybody and having the necessary discipline to carry it out and not waste effort on irrelevant activities. Managers at every level are under constant pressure to compromise – to trade-off longer-term strategically relevant activities for shorter-term concerns needing urgent attention. It is the task of strategic leaders to teach others in an organization about a chosen strategy, especially in how to guide priorities in daily management decision-making.

References

Chesbrough, H., & Rosenbloom, R. (2002), The role of the business model in capturing value from innovation: Evidence from Xerox corporation's technology, *Industrial and Corporate Change*, 11, 529–555.

Henderson, B. D. (1974), The experience curve reviewed, *Perspectives*, the Boston Consulting Group, //www.bcg.com

Porter, M. E. (1980), *Competitive Strategy: Techniques for Analyzing Industries and Competitors*, Boston, MA: Free Press.

Porter, M. E. (1985), *Competitive Advantage: Creating and Sustaining Superior Performance*, New York: Free Press.

7 Corporate-level strategy

Essential summary

Corporate-level strategy is a corporate centre's strategy for managing a multi-business organization; it is concerned with the growth and development of multiple businesses and thus works at a higher level compared to single business strategy.

The *product-expansion grid* is Ansoff's matrix used to show four main directions of growth using the terms market penetration, product development, market development, and diversification.

Prospectors, analyzers, defenders, and *reactors* are terms used by Miles and Snow to characterize distinct organizational approaches to strategy based on how organizations choose markets, decide on the means of producing products and services, organize and manage work.

Mergers and acquisitions (M&A) are agreements made by organizations to integrate their operations into common ownership, while acquisitions occur when one organization buys a controlling interest in another.

Vertical and horizontal integration describe the direction of growth of an organization's operations, either vertically along a distribution chain and a supply chain or horizontally through the introduction of complementary products and services or by acquiring a rival with similar offers.

Strategic portfolio analysis is a group of units or companies managed by a corporate centre as a portfolio of distinct businesses. The Growth-Share Matrix and the Boston Box are examples.

Related diversification happens when a corporation's businesses have some characteristics in common which allow a corporate parent to build synergies that benefit all the businesses that otherwise would not exist.

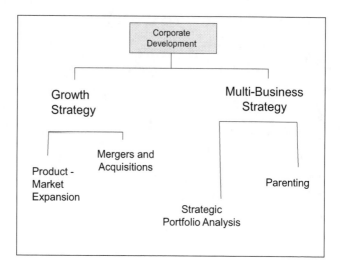

Figure 7.1 Strategies for corporate development

Corporate-level strategy is a corporate centre's approach for strategically managing a multi-business group of organizations. These are of a sufficient size to operate in more than one industry and in several markets. A corporate centre is typically a centrally located headquarters. A concern for any organization but especially for one made up of several businesses is how to strategically manage the whole so that the different organizational parts work together effectively to achieve strategic purpose. One of the fathers of strategic management, Igor Ansoff (1965), emphasized the importance of corporate synergy, which he called a '2 + 2 = 5 effect', in which an organization's parts have a combined performance that is greater than the sum of its parts.

Many multi-business organizations have businesses that could exist independently. However, some businesses do better if they are grouped with other businesses under a single corporate management. In this instance the corporate centre creates sufficient extra value that more than offsets the centre's costs. Figure 7.1 outlines two broad approaches for corporate development.

The product-expansion grid

Ansoff suggests there are four main directions to take in expanding an organization's markets and products, which he illustrates with his product-market expansion grid (sometimes called the growth vector matrix) (see

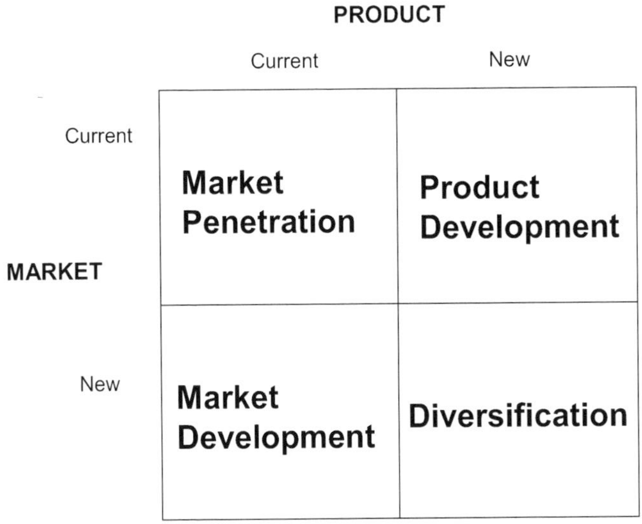

PRODUCT

	Current	New
Current **MARKET**	**Market Penetration**	**Product Development**
New	**Market Development**	**Diversification**

Figure 7.2 Ansoff's product/market expansion grid

Figure 7.2). Four directions of expansion are possible: market penetration, market development, product development, and diversification.

Market penetration involves growing current business – using the existing product range to increase an organization's share of its existing markets. This is the least risky strategy of the four options. An organization, for example, should be able to understand its existing customers and use existing activities to encourage them to buy more. Prospective customers, who may currently be buying from rivals, can also be encouraged.

Market development introduces an organization's existing products and services into new markets. The move into new areas usually requires good research and marketing strategy to provide an initial entry and target segments. There are likely to be significant potential differences between existing and new markets, so caution and understanding are required.

Product development introduces new products and services into existing markets. Ideas for new products typically come from understanding the needs and behaviour of existing customers, but the risk of new product failure is minimized if innovation is piloted or developed with existing customers.

Diversification involves introducing new products and services into new markets. This is the riskiest option. An organization has to take time to develop new resources and understand unfamiliar products and market behaviour. For large organizations, inorganic growth offers an attractive way forward to gain the necessary expertise if investors support the move with new finance to cover the costs of acquisitions.

Prospectors, analyzers, defenders, and reactors

In their influential book *Organization Strategy, Structure, and Process*, Raymond E. Miles and Charles C. Snow (1978) argue that strategy is influenced by how organizations decide to address three fundamental problems. The first is entrepreneurial how to choose a general and target market; the second is an engineering matter – how to decide the most appropriate means to offer products and services; and the third is an administrative issue – how to organize and manage the work. How organizations address these problems identifies four distinct types of organization: prospectors, analyzers, defenders, and reactors.

Prospectors

These diversify and promote a visionary strategy. Organizational learning is exploratory, seeking new competitive positions. Prospectors are characterized by flexibility; coordination and facilitation are important. The nature of planning is broad and sensitive to external changes. Prospectors are likely to be first-movers.

Defenders

These target a narrow market and concentrate mainly on the engineering issue of how to produce products and services to deliver value. Review and continuous improvement are important, and organizations stick to a core mission. Control is centralized and sensitive to internal conditions. Defenders are more functionally-based with finance and production dominant.

Analyzers

These use market development, review, and planning and implement strategic projects. Their characteristics are a combination of prospector and defender approaches, aiming to avoid excessive risks and do well in the delivery of new products and service. Analyzers are represented by larger companies, which cover a variety of markets and industries.

Reactors

These use market penetration, tending to use short-term expediency and crisis management. The strategy is to avoid being overwhelmed. Their response to change is typically inconsistent and inappropriate since a mismatch exists in the three fundamental problems. Reactors often have little control over their external environment.

Miles and Snow argue that an organization's strategy, structure, and processes should be consistent, although they suggest different strategies can be used by a single organization for different projects. They argue that no single type of strategy is best; rather, what determines the ultimate success of an organization is the fact of establishing and sustaining a systematic strategy which takes into account the organization's environment, technology, and structure. In other words, pick a strategy and stick to it.

The Miles and Snow scheme can be linked to the product-market growth grid (see Figure 7.3). A prospector strategy is associated with diversification; an analyzer, with market development; a defender, with product development; and a reactor, with market penetration. The arrows in the figure indicate a potential cycle of strategy movement: when an organization diversifies, it moves afterwards to an analyzer position, then to defender and reactor positions. It then becomes necessary to adopt a new prospector

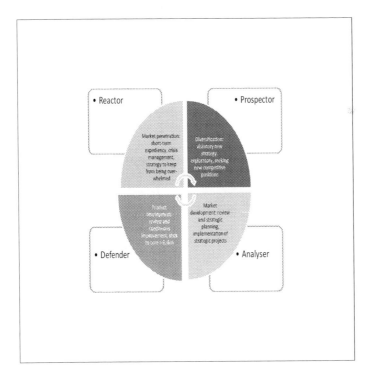

Figure 7.3 Ansoff, Miles, and Snow

approach to find and implement a more radical strategy to retake the initiative in the industry – known as a turnaround strategy.

Mergers and acquisitions (M&A)

A merger is an agreement between two organizations to combine and integrate their operations under a common ownership. A merger of equals is unusual since one of the organizations is usually more dominant, and its management is likely to be favoured in post-merger negotiations and reorganization. An acquisition happens when one organization buys a controlling interest in another to create a larger entity or, more rarely, to restructure the acquisition with a view to reselling later at a profit. Surveys carried out by the management consultancy McKinsey and Company suggest the most common rationale for M&A is to acquire new products, intellectual property, and capabilities. Other reasons include a need to incubate new businesses, enter new geographies, and acquire increased scale.

The direction of integration: vertical and horizontal

Expansion in an organization's activities in an industry takes two directions: vertical and horizontal. Vertical integration is the expansion of an organization's activities up a distribution chain or down the supply chain. Horizontal integration is the expansion of an organization's activities sideways in an industry, achieved by acquiring rivals in the same part of the supply chain.

Backward vertical integration enables an organization to control some of the resources that are used as inputs in the production of its products and services. Forward vertical integration up the distribution chain enables more control of the distribution centres and retailers. However, an alternative approach to controlling an industry's participants in a supply chain is to influence their bargaining power through purchasing power. This is often a preferred strategy if an organization wants to spread its risk over several suppliers.

Horizontal integration occurs when competitors that offer similar or complementary products and services are taken over and merged with an organization's existing activities. With time industries tend to become more concentrated as horizontal integration activity narrows down the number of rivals.

M&A is a quick way to increase the scale of operations and market power. It can also take an acquiring organization into new markets and industries, and M&A is classically associated with new and expanding industries and markets. However, the results of M&A activity are often problematic. Success requires a clear consolidation strategy before an acquisition is completed. To achieve synergy the integration process needs to be prompt and decisive once the financial transaction is over. A basic understanding of an acquired organization is needed on the part of senior management of the acquiring organization. The most successful mergers have been between organizations with an already established history of partnerships, such as joint ventures or alliances.

A minority of mergers and acquisitions may show positive results in the years immediately following the completion of deals. M&A typically create uncertainty: top salespeople became recruitment targets for rivals, post-merger redundancies damage morale, and consumers are sensitive to signs that product or service quality is slipping. While restructuring and cost-cutting can boost short-term earnings, longer-term progress is difficult if management is damaged or stagnates.

Philippe Haspeslagh and David Jemison (1991) suggest the degree of strategic interdependence between acquired and acquiring organizations depends upon the expected value it creates. This rests on value from sharing resources at the operating level – a transfer of functional skills by moving people or sharing knowledge or a transfer of managers to improve control and insight. Extra value can be obtained by combining benefits created by leveraging resources (such as borrowing capacity, added purchasing power, and greater market power).

Care must be taken not to damage the value of an acquired organization, and a judgement is necessary about the need for the appropriate degree of required organizational autonomy. This is determined by asking whether autonomy is essential for the acquired organization to preserve the strategic capability that it was bought for, how much autonomy is necessary, and which areas autonomy is important in.

Haspeslagh and Jemison suggest four approaches (see Figure 7.4): absorption, when the acquisition should be fully integrated into the acquiring organization; preservation, when the acquired organization should be given full autonomy; symbiosis, when integration should be gradual and existing organizational boundaries should be permeable but maintained; and holding, when there is no intention to integrate, except for financial transfers and risk sharing.

An important aspect of M&A is cultural fit, where the organizational culture of an acquisition should be compatible with that of the acquiring organization. It is relatively easy to evaluate strategic fit since organizations can analyze whether two organizations are complementary in terms of geography, products, customers, or technologies. Cultural fit is difficult because organizations have unique and often very different ways of doing business. In particular, they have different strategic resources that are difficult for different organizations to identify and understand. An acquired organization's

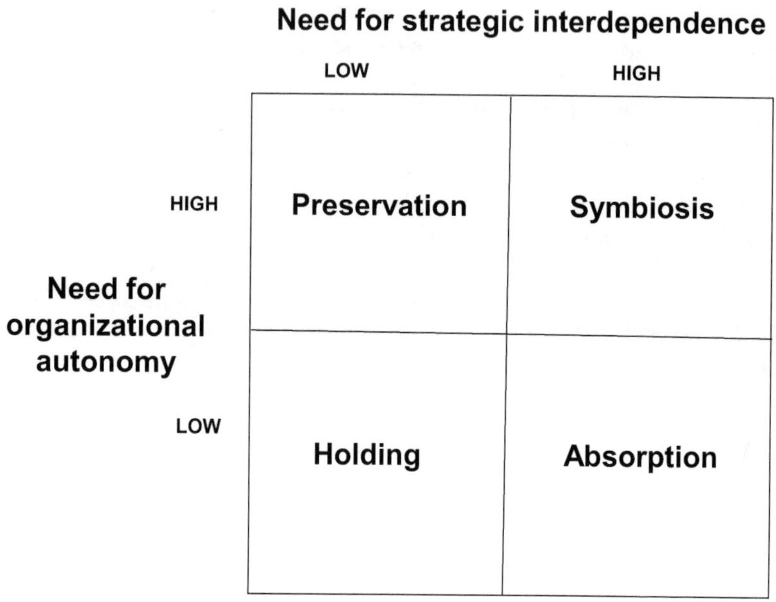

Need for strategic interdependence

	LOW	HIGH
HIGH	Preservation	Symbiosis
LOW	Holding	Absorption

Need for organizational autonomy

Figure 7.4 The degree of consolidation and integration

culture, say, a sales culture, can fight the culture of the acquiring organization, say, an engineering company.

Strategic portfolio analysis

Unrelated diversification is the involvement of an organization in different industries, while related diversification occurs typically within one industry. Unrelated diversification offers contrasting products and services that have little or no relation to each other. While moving into unfamiliar industries and markets has great risks, once established it can spread risks across different trading conditions and provide security for the organization as a whole. The most extreme form of unrelated diversification is the conglomerate organization. During the middle years of the twentieth century there was a strong growth in conglomerates.

Many of these add value for their financial stakeholders by imposing radical rationalization and aggressive management on acquisitions. When an acquisition is bought cheaply and its parts are restructured and sold off profitability, the process is called asset stripping. In recent times large conglomerates have appeared in the emerging economies of Asia, where industrial groups had been encouraged by government policy that limits foreign competition and encourages indigenous economic development. However, in general, conglomerates are less favourably regarded today than they were, but many of the world's largest corporations are diversified organizations, many of which have been around for many decades.

The strategic management of diversified organizations is primarily carried out as a portfolio of strategic business units. This is called strategic portfolio analysis, which is used at a corporate level by executives and central management to appraise the performance of a group of corporate businesses. It is primarily a corporate framework to manage a set of distinct investments. It is not meant to be a vehicle for analyzing the internal management of the businesses, although it can be used to identify problem businesses, which may then lead to corporate interventions. The best-known portfolio approach is the Boston Consulting Group's Growth-Share Matrix (sometimes called the Boston Box) (Henderson, 1984).

The growth-share matrix

The Growth-Share Matrix was introduced in 1970 by the Boston Consulting Group to categorize businesses by their overall market growth and market share (see Figure 7.5). The principle is to rank and review the performance of businesses in an analogous way to a portfolio of investments. Some businesses will be starting; others, growing. Some will be stable, while some

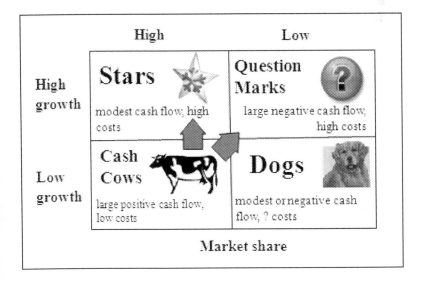

Figure 7.5 The growth-share matrix

will be in decline. A balance between these is maintained: the businesses that have potential tomorrow can be funded by transferring money from the successful breadwinners of today.

Cash cows

Businesses classed as cash cows have a high market share in a slow-growing market, typically in a mature industry. These will generate cash in excess of the amount needed to invest to maintain the health of the business, so an excess is creamed off to provide investment funds for stars and question marks. Of course, a cash cow business is likely to be unhappy to see its revenue moved if it is prevented from diversifying itself from expanding into new business. From the perspective of the corporate whole, however, the principle is that slow-growing but cash-rich businesses should provide the investment necessary for the future.

Stars

Stars have a high market share and are in growing markets. The expectation is that these businesses will become the cash cows of tomorrow, but for the present they are likely to be hungry for more investment funds than they can self-generate. The principle is to grow star businesses as fast as possible by removing resource constraints; for instance, to invest in added capacity ahead of demand.

Question marks

Question mark businesses have a low market share but are located in fast-growing markets. A question mark business is sometimes called a problem child because typically it does not generate investment funds, and the future of the business is uncertain. A question mark business has the potential to become a star, but it is likely to be very cash-hungry in its early stages of market development. Corporations are typically involved in a number of promising but unproven businesses, particularly in unfamiliar industries. The principle is to be prepared to move resources into expanding businesses, but at the same time noting that caution is necessary as well.

Dogs

Dog businesses have a low market share and are in low-growth markets. If they add little value to the corporate whole, they are divested or closed down. These may be pet businesses in that they once contributed significantly to the success of the corporation, so psychologically it can be difficult for sentimental owners to close them down. It may be prudent to keep a dog alive if it blocks existing competition (like a guard dog); complements other businesses (guide dog); or creates customers at the bottom of the product's range who may trade up to high-value products later on (sheep dog). However, the principle is that these businesses should be terminated as soon as conditions allow.

The advantage of a growth-share matrix is that it is a straight-forward approach for identifying the most attractive corporate businesses in which to put cash. It helps senior managers to compare the businesses on their competiveness. Of course, cash flow is influenced by more than simply market share and industry growth, and many external considerations are ignored that could have a significant impact upon decisions. The approach puts an emphasis on the internal competition for funds. It is not meant to be deterministic, and it is only a framework to help guide decisions, so it is useful for corporate-level periodic reviews. The portfolio concept has been used for a long time, but its form is generally modified to suit a particular organization, of which the best-known example is the GE-McKinsey nine-box matrix, which is based on industry attractiveness and business strength.

Strategic business unit (SBU)

When conglomerate organizations are structured into businesses that have a strong degree of strategic independence from the corporate centre, they are called strategic business units (SBUs). Typically a SBU has a general manager who is assisted by a staff that includes the functional heads working in the business, which are middle managers in the sense they report to senior executives at the corporate headquarters or centre. However, corporate executives are not directly involved with running the strategic management of the SBU; instead, their role is to evaluate performance and manage the overall allocation of resources of the group.

If the degree of strategic independence is high, a SBU will have its own business generic strategy for its industry, along with distinctive organizational cultures and competencies. The insularity of the SBU portfolio structure means that individual SBUs can be added or divested by the corporate centre without any significant knock-on effects for the strategy and organizational cultures of the other SBUs in the portfolio. This brings a degree of flexibility that allows a corporate centre to move the group's interests easily between industries without integration worries and much dislocation. The great advantage of a diversified corporation is that it spreads risk if businesses are located in different industries and markets.

Related diversification

However, since the 1980s there has been a shift in strategic thinking away from unrelated diversification towards related diversification. An example from the resource-based view is Prahalad and Hamel's (1990) concept of related core products. These are areas of organization-specific expertise and resources that can be configured to produce a range of final products and services for different and unconnected markets. Prahalad and Hamel use the example of Canon and its use of technical competencies in optics as a core product to serve markets as diverse as cameras, copiers, and semiconductor equipment. This is possible because Canon's people work together effectively in common ways. Canon's competitive advantage is an internal capability not easily seen or understood by its rivals.

A company is likened to a tree (see Figure 7.6). Its competencies are the organization's roots, its core products are the trunk, the corporate businesses in their different industries and markets are the tree's separate branches, and the leaves and fruit are its end-products. When businesses in a portfolio are related, a corporate centre is able to identify operational synergies, distinctive skills, and specific strengths.

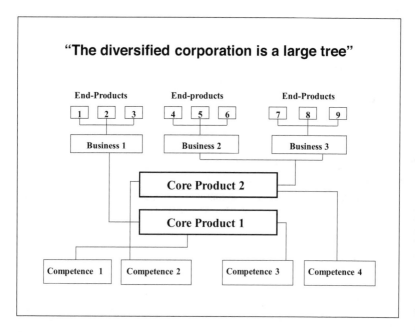

Figure 7.6 Related diversification as a corporate tree

Michael Goold, Andrew Campbell, and Marcus Alexander (1994) contrast unrelated to related diversification strategies and introduce the concept of corporate parenting. This is how a corporate centre acts as a parent to the corporate businesses by nurturing and growing them synergistically as dependent entities. Parenting aims to create a unique fit between a corporation's capabilities and the CSFs for each of the individual businesses, and by so doing the corporate parent creates value. Some corporations organize their strategy around the needs of the businesses so that the direction of strategy formation is outside-in from the businesses rather than from the centre out. However, parenting styles differ.

Goold and Campbell (1991) offer a typology of three broad parenting styles – financial control, strategic planning, and strategic control. Financial control involves a portfolio approach. This is less about parenting and more about the centre achieving a better investment performance. SBUs manage their strategy within tight financial targets set by the centre. Strategic planning emphasizes linkages, where the centre coordinates and reviews strategy. The centre sets tight financial and strategic targets. There is some attempt to create links between the different businesses to create competitive advantage. Strategic control is based on the management of the core business. The centre drives strategy around the development of important synergies and competencies, and there are strong coordinating actions and linkages between the businesses.

References

Ansoff, H. I. (1965), *Corporate Strategy: An Analytic Approach to Business Policy for Growth and Expansion*, London: McGraw-Hill, revised 1987.

Goold, M., & Campbell, A. (1991), *Strategies and Style: The Role of the Centre in Managing Diversified Corporation*, London: Blackwell.

Goold, M., Campbell, A., & Alexander, M. (1994), *Corporate Level Strategy: Creating Value in the Multibusiness Company*, New York: John Wiley & Sons.

Haspeslagh, P. C., & Jemison, D. B. (1991), *Managing Acquisitions: Creating Value through Corporate Renewal*, New York: Free Press.

Henderson, B. D. (1984), *The Logic of Business Strategy*, New York: Ballinger Publishing.

Miles, R. E., & Snow, C. C. (1978), *Organizational Strategy, Structure and Process*, London: McGraw-Hill.

Prahalad, C. A., & Hamel, G. (1990), The core competence of the corporation, *Harvard Business Review*, May-June, 79–91.

8   Global-level strategy

Essential summary

Global level strategy is the organization's strategy for the management of its operations across multi-national borders.

Porter's diamond is a model to show how the competitive advantage of nations is based on local regional advantages.

Strategies for international markets include multi-domestic, global, international, and transnational.

Micro multinationals are small organizations that maintain a hub in a domestic economy but use the Internet to reach customers who are spread out across global markets.

Strategic alliances and partnerships are formal and informal associations and collaborations between independent organizations.

Global-level strategy is an organization's strategic management of its operations across multi-national borders. Typically, these organizations are multinational corporations (MNCs) and play an important part in globalization. This is a phenomenon of changing commonalties and differences associated with a worldwide perception that the world is becoming smaller, more alike, and more interconnected.

Globalization is a growing world phenomenon of connections, associations, differences, and commonalities which influence national markets and international industries. Human activity and business are converging and becoming more interconnected all over the world. It is the most important change phenomenon of our time and is inextricably tied up with the great international debates about climate change and the economic management of our planet. The pressures to internationalize approaches to organizational management are very strong; however, success in international markets may begin with a strong base at home.

The competitive advantage of nations

Michael Porter (1990) investigated 20 industrial sectors in 12 countries and found that many internationally leading industries were clustered in geographical regions. His research pointed to the importance of both developing and nurturing a geographical concentration of suppliers and specialized resources and balancing between an industry's home-based activities and those dispersed abroad. Thus, an organization's competitive advantage in part depends upon local advantages that cluster as a regionally localized industry. Porter's diamond illustrates the primary drivers of a nation's competitive strength (see Figure 8.1).

Strategy, structure, and rivalry

The intensity of domestic competition works to compel organizations to work for improved productivity and innovation. An important factor is a country's capital market. When relatively short-term returns to investment are expected, industries with short investment cycles are encouraged – computers and cinema are examples. In countries where the investment cycle is longer, investment favours more radical technology, such as Toyota's hybrid car, which the company started to develop in the 1990s.

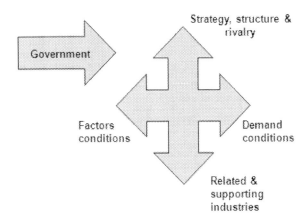

Figure 8.1 Porter's diamond for the competitive advantage of nations

Demand conditions

The presence of demanding and sophisticated customers will spur greater efforts and increase competitiveness. Domestic industries are encouraged by open competition – since this raises expectations about the standard of service and products a market wants – and spurs local organizations to innovate and improve.

Related and supporting industries

A sufficient density of related and supporting organizations, especially the proximity of distributors, suppliers, and other organizations that facilitate an industry's activities, provides an infrastructure that is favourable as a springboard for competitive advantage.

Factor conditions

Factor conditions encourage the development of specialized resources, including skilled labour and capital, which are customized to suit local industry needs. They do not include general-use resources that are usually always available and cannot be said to provide a distinctive competitive advantage. A clustering of similar organizations can foster an environment of both cooperation and competition conducive to creativity and the development of new ideas. Competition acts as a driver, while cooperation provides insights that can be exploited.

The role of government

The purpose of national governments, in the view of Porter, is to provide and facilitate economic conditions that act as a catalyst and encourage enterprise. Thus, local rivalry is stimulated by policy that limits collusion and promotes free competition. Government is a peripheral influence since the role of government can be good or bad. However, policy interventions can work well to build infrastructure, develop specialist resources, and boost investment to encourage innovation. Peter Drucker (1955) compared the success of Japan to the failure of the United Kingdom to support innovative industries that would have maintained the country's technological leadership.

The diamond model is not meant to be a practical strategic management tool to help specific organizations compete more effectively. Porter designed it to help understand why a nation is successful in some industries and not in others. This can help strategists understand how their organizations can use the resources and networks in their home-base to build a firmer foundation for success in global markets.

Strategies for international markets

The effects of globalization on the competitive advantage of nations with developed economies have been profound, particularly for manufacturing industries. Emerging economies offer an important cost advantage for large international multinationals, and many have moved parts of their production to low-wage Asian countries. While the supply-side advantages are high, on the demand side, the size and growth of markets in emergent economies also offer scope for growth that would be impossible in domestic markets.

There are four types of strategy for global organizations, depending upon the strength of pressure to keep the costs of economic integration low and the strength of the need to be responsive to local and national conditions: multi-domestic, global, international, and transnational (see Figure 8.2) (Bartlett C. and Beamish P., 2018).

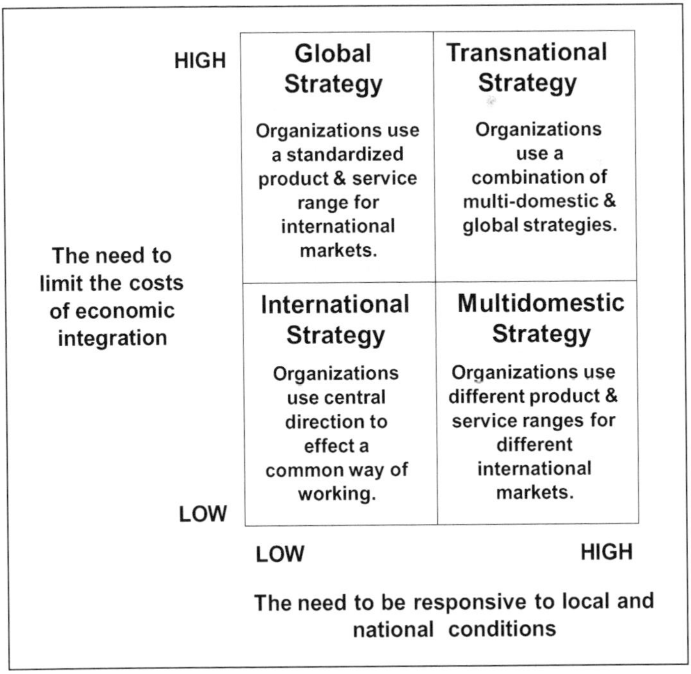

	LOW	HIGH
HIGH	**Global Strategy** — Organizations use a standardized product & service range for international markets.	**Transnational Strategy** — Organizations use a combination of multi-domestic & global strategies.
LOW	**International Strategy** — Organizations use central direction to effect a common way of working.	**Multidomestic Strategy** — Organizations use different product & service ranges for different international markets.

The need to limit the costs of economic integration (vertical). The need to be responsive to local and national conditions (horizontal).

Figure 8.2 Four types of strategy for international markets

Multi-domestic strategy

Multi-domestic strategy involves using different products and services to suit different markets in different countries. This approach is based on knowledge that markets in different countries or regional parts of the world are distinctly different from each other. A simple transfer of an existing strategy that has been effective in a domestic market or another foreign market may not necessarily work for a new country. Thus, strategy should be sensitive to the local domestic environment and take into account characteristics such as behavioural patterns and attitudes and any other relevant local factors, including food preferences and religious customs.

The solution is to develop a strategy that recognizes local conditions, even though the overall organizational costs of integration to the organization may be high if it is necessary to give local managers responsibilities and considerable autonomy for making strategic and operating decisions. The need to respond to local conditions to maximize revenue takes precedence and compensates for extra costs. Expansion into foreign markets may involve the acquisition of companies that are familiar with local conditions. This has risks if there is a clash of organizational cultures or the distant parent organization is thought to be too slow to support local decisions. The intervention of corporate management may also be misinterpreted at a local level as uninformed interference.

Global strategy

Global strategy involves the use of a standardized product and service range for all of an organization's international markets. This brings economies of scale from centralized production, distribution, and marketing, and it suits situations where consumer lifestyles and tastes converge, as is sometimes the case for global brands.

A brand is a name or label that incorporates a visual design and image and differentiates an organization's products and services from rivals. Various positive attributes are associated with the brand through communication media and advertising to create value that goes beyond the intrinsic functional value of the product or service bought. When branding is effective, it offers attractive price premiums to the producer and creates strong loyalty to the brand from the customer.

Brands are important to global strategy as they signify a standardized offer and a consistent promise of benefits regardless of where purchases are made. Global brands reach across the world even though many of them were originally domestic in conception, but in the wake of changes in global media they have been able to move into a new dimension. International businesses should target cities in emergent markets where more affluent consumers are located, and the intensity of competition is typically higher than in a country at large.

International strategy

International strategy uses central direction to facilitate common ways of working across an organization's subsidiaries. The focus is on a multinational's centre when corporate businesses are aligned around a common corporate culture and shared values, management philosophies, and business methodologies. This reflects the idea that related diversification depends upon the corporation's core products rather than its end-products and services. Thus, international strategy is focused on enterprise-wide objectives managed from the centre. These organizations are likely to develop new practices centrally and diffuse them to subsidiaries; policies and incentives are maintained consistently from country to country. While foreign experience is a prerequisite for senior management, the aim is to build a common corporate culture across all the businesses.

Transnational strategy

Transnational strategy is used to exploit markets in different countries by a mixture of multi-domestic and global strategies. Local markets are globally accessible, but they have different cultural conditions that require a regionally customized approach. In this, the interests of the greater organization must be balanced with the needs of local management and its need to make local strategic decisions.

One form of transnational strategy is based on flexible manufacturing, which uses common production platforms that facilitate the use of the same type of modular components worldwide. The best examples belong to the car industry. During the 1980s and 1990s, General Motors (GM) and Ford both sought to develop a world car. They aimed to gain economies of scale by selling the same car everywhere rather than developing vehicles separately for each region. In the end, finding out that roads are different across the world and demand different things from cars, they abandoned this ideal in favour of platforms (or architectures) designed to produce a common group of basic models; the models are varied at local points of assembly and marketed in ways to suit local national conditions. Car companies centralize their R&D while dispersing manufacturing to relatively low-cost assembly units and suppliers.

Micro-multinationals

A micro-multinational is a small to midsize manufacturer or service provider that maintains a hub in a domestic economy, while its international customers are spread out across the world. A micro-multinational is typically located in a niche sector of an industry where novel technologies are used that are esoteric yet vital to a larger industry. Competitors are usually few in number. Before the advent of the Internet, organizations had to be large to gain a global reach, but this is no longer true. From startup, entrepreneurs can access international markets at little initial cost. While many of these have experienced chequered histories, some of the most successful have become very big indeed and are household names – for example, Amazon and eBay.

Strategies for local companies in emerging markets

Niraj Dawar and Tony Frost (1999) have put forward a strategic framework for local companies to assess their competitive strength in an emerging market, which is based on the strength of globalization pressures and the degree to which a company's assets are transferable internationally (see Figure 8.3).

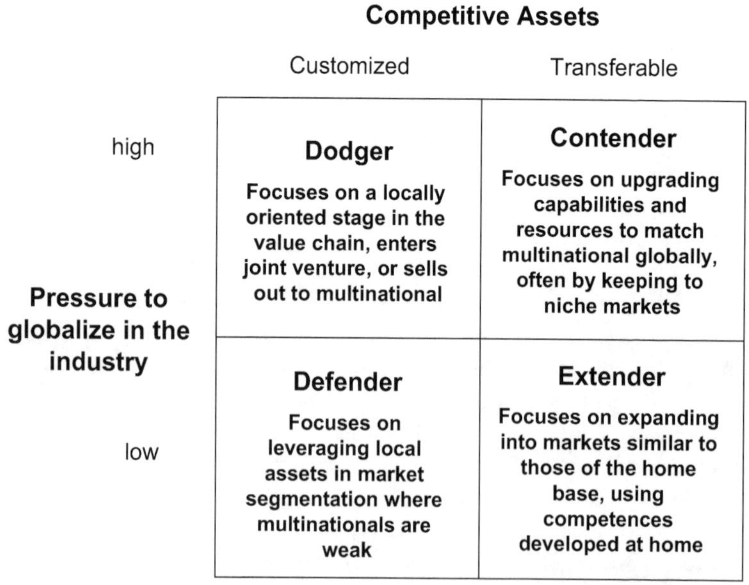

Competitive Assets

	Customized	Transferable
high	**Dodger** Focuses on a locally oriented stage in the value chain, enters joint venture, or sells out to multinational	**Contender** Focuses on upgrading capabilities and resources to match multinational globally, often by keeping to niche markets
low	**Defender** Focuses on leveraging local assets in market segmentation where multinationals are weak	**Extender** Focuses on expanding into markets similar to those of the home base, using competences developed at home

Pressure to globalize in the industry (row label spanning between high and low)

Figure 8.3 Positioning for emergent market companies

Dodger strategy

A local company might follow a dodger strategy if its resources are customized to local conditions and if it receives strong competitive pressure internationally. This involves working alongside a multinational, perhaps by offering local services or entering into a joint venture. In the early stages of increased competition, local companies are likely to have a low-cost advantage, but once this diminishes it may be preferable to sell out to a foreign company.

Defender

If pressure from international businesses is low, a defender strategy is more appropriate. A local company can target market segments where multinational competition is weak. A local company may have developed low-cost mass-market brands positioned around regional beliefs about traditional ingredients that multinationals ignore.

Contender

When competitive pressure from international organizations is high, local companies can follow a contender strategy by upgrading their resources and capabilities to suit relatively small and specialized markets in other regions or countries. Niche markets are generally left alone by larger international organizations.

Extender

With low levels of competition, an extender strategy to transfer domestic products and services to similar markets offers opportunities for expansion into other regions and countries.

National cultures

There is evidence that organizations active in different countries can be successful in building a one-company culture in that business methodologies and management philosophies do transfer between countries. This is important to organizations that take a resource-based view of competitive advantage. However, the national culture of management is likely to influence management style, and this influences organizational culture. Geert Hofstede's (1980) pioneering research into national cultures and management suggested that there are no universal management styles. He identified five dimensions of national culture that influence how organizations are managed:

1   Power distance: the degree of inequality a national culture considers normal – it seems to be greatest for Latino, Asian, African, and Arab communities and low for northern Europeans.
2   Individualism versus collectivism: the extent to which it is appropriate for people to look after themselves and be cared for – developed countries have the greatest individualism.
3   Masculinity versus femininity: the acceptable balance between dominance, assertiveness, and acquisition compared to regard for people, feelings, and quality of life – Nordic countries have the lowest difference, while masculinity is very high in Japan.
4   Uncertainty avoidance: the degree of preference for structured versus unstructured situations – it is high for Latin American countries, southern Europe, and Eastern Europe, German-speaking countries, and Japan; it is low in Anglo-American and Nordic countries and in China.
5   Long-term versus short-term orientation: persistence to reach a future rather than live in the present, follow tradition, and other social obligations – long-term orientations are found in China and Japan but are low in Anglo-American, Islamic, African, and Latin American countries.

Such cultural diversity is associated with differences in the nature of social and economic institutions between countries. This is likely to have strong influences on how large organizations, especially multinationals, organize and manage their strategic management across borders. At the time of the 2008 global financial crisis much was made about a crisis of capitalism, in particular about which are the most appropriate forms or varieties of capitalism for global-level strategy.

Varieties of capitalism

Economists Peter Hall and David Soskice (2001) make an important observation that the nature of capitalism in an economy depends upon the strategic interactions and complementarities between institutions and organizations. These provide the prevailing mode of coordination of resources that firms will use for their strategic management. They identify two contrasting modes: a liberal market economy, where an emphasis is given to competitive market arrangements; and a coordinated market economy, where collaborative institutional relations act to reduce uncertainty on longer-term purpose.

In a liberal market economy the near-term needs of a firm's financial stakeholders are a primary concern. These are typically equity shareholders.

A priority for executives is to maintain a level of dividend and a high share price that will protect the firm from a hostile takeover. Government policy is designed to encourage free competition. In a coordinated market economy the participation of stakeholders, such as employer associations, trade unions, and professional networks, is important for cross-sharing support and ideas. The regulatory systems in these economies work to facilitate a free movement of information and industry collaboration.

The US, UK, Australia, Canada, New Zealand, and Ireland are recognized as liberal market economies, while central and northern European countries and Japan are identified as coordinated market economies. Hall and Soskice point out how the economies of the United States and the United Kingdom are characterized by a free market ethos, while the German economy is characterized by close cooperative relations between firms, banks, owners, and employees. Similarly, Japan's economy depends on a coordinated partnership of professional societies, banking and industrial groups, and government agencies.

The economic success of China has caused many observers to see state capitalism as a challenge to free market economies. China is reported to provide aggressive financial support to its companies to invest overseas and sign deals in sectors such as energy and raw materials to build new multinationals while securing supplies of strategic commodities. There is also pressure on foreign multinationals to transfer knowledge of important technologies in return for access to the Chinese market.

Strategic alliances and partnerships

Strategic alliances and partnerships are formal and informal associations and collaborations between independently owned organizations. A formal alliance involves a legally binding collaboration between two organizations to work to a specified purpose, which may involve a major project and shared resources. It can involve forming another independent organization, such as a joint venture; this involves establishing a legally separate company in which the partners take agreed equity stakes. Agreements are made to establish a common purpose, standards, and contractual arrangements, covering such matters as licensing, franchises, distribution rights, and manufacturing agreements. Informal alliances may be entered into with customers who have major accounts, key distributors, preferred suppliers, major institutional shareholders, and other stakeholders.

The reasons for alliances and partnerships are varied and numerous. Often it is to share knowledge about new technologies in return for access to markets. Alliances also help organizations to find out about another company's management approaches or about unfamiliar markets. They can help to reduce the cost of capital and spread risk, and sometimes they are a more acceptable form of market entry to regulators. However, they are not without challenges. In a Chinese study of joint ventures, it was found that the main difficulties that foreign organizations have had with their Chinese partners were cultural differences and communication problems (Tian, 2016).

References

Bartlett, C., & Beamish, P. (2018), *Transnational Management: Text, Cases and Readings*, London: McGraw-Hill.

Dawar, N., & Frost, T. (1999), Competing with Giants: Survival strategies for local companies, *Harvard Business Review*, March-April, 119–129.

Drucker, P. F. (1955), *The Practice of Management*, London: Heinemann Butterworth.

Hall, P., & Soskice, D. (eds.) (2001), *Varieties of Capitalism: The Institutional Foundations of Comparative Advantage*, Oxford: Oxford University Press.

Hofstede, G. (1980), *Culture's Consequences: International Differences in Work-Related Values*, London: Sage Publications.

Porter, M. E. (1990), *The Competitive Advantage of Nations*, New York: Free Press.

Tian, X. (2016), *Managing International Business in China*, Cambridge: Cambridge University Press.

9 Strategy implementation

Essential summary

Strategy implementation is the putting in place of necessary organizational structure and systems to carry out strategic management.

Organizing is central: the last twenty years has seen a shift away from formal bureaucratic structures to favour ideas about organizing to innovate and design work that facilitates teamwork and process management.

Organizational structure includes four basic types – functional, product, matrix, and regional structure.

A *process* is a sequence of organized tasks to deliver an objective.

Cross-functional working involves teams with individuals who come from different functional areas of an organization working together to meet an objective.

McKinsey's 7S framework is a conceptual framework of seven interrelated variables for organizing the management of change, which emphasizes organizational values in addition to strategy, structure, and systems.

Strategy implementation puts in place and organizes structure and systems for an organization's strategic management. The most important part is the design of appropriate organizational structure (Daft, 2012). Structure is the organization of effort into a coherent and working entity. For nearly all organizations a characterizing feature is a formal hierarchy of responsibilities. This enables centralized decision-making and orders the number of organizational levels and the direction of reporting. Broadly, there are four groupings of structural forms: functional, product, area, and matrix (see figure 9.1). The lines between the boxes show the main reporting paths between the different parts.

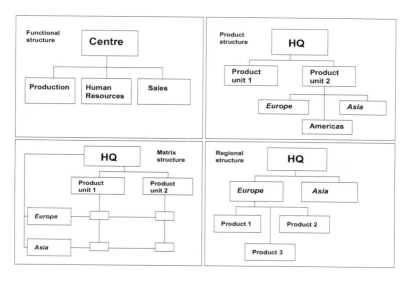

Figure 9.1 Four basic types of organizational form

Functional structure is the division of work into specialist activities, such as departments that specialize in purchasing, manufacturing, marketing, finance, and so on. This specialization is required so that teams and individuals develop expertise to be able to carry out work effectively. To work as an overall system, the separate parts must be coordinated effectively by a centre; the structure is hierarchical since the centre at the top of the organization administers the overall design of the transformation process.

As organizations grow in size they typically become multi-product and multi-market enterprises and group their activities into divisions based on products and geographical regions. These are organized into functional activities with their own coordinating centre and are typically under the control of a general manager, whose team reports to the organization's headquarters. Multi-divisional structure of this kind is called M-form organization.

The M-form enables each division to specialize on particular products (or brands) or on a distinct regional market. The divisions allow organizations to remain close to customers so that they are able to identify and respond quickly to the changing needs of the markets. The overall coordination of the divisions is managed by executives at headquarters. A weakness is that divisions can find it difficult to collaborate with each other when inter-divisional and inter-departmental projects are necessary.

In cases where inter-divisional projects are central to an organization's core business, organizations may use a matrix structure. Project teams and units are organized to report jointly to product and regional management. Matrix organizing is sometimes difficult to manage because of an inherent tension between the different interests of product and regional management. A project manager struggles with the difficulties of joint accountability and authority, which in the matrix organization are often ambiguous.

The nature of approaches to thinking about appropriate strategy varies with differences in organizational hierarchy. Alfred Chandler (1962), an economic historian and one of the first to write about organization and strategy, thought strategy should be made at an organization's centre, while divisions should only be involved with operations. The notion that strategy is distinct from operations is a central one for classical strategic management. This is the idea that strategic planning is primarily a central and long-term function, while its implementation is carried out through shorter-term management control and operations by middle management.

Over the last twenty years the reverse has happened as many large corporations made their organizations flatter to reduce the numbers of middle managers and the size and number of centralized functions at a corporate headquarters. In part this reflects a move towards more customer-based organizing based on business processes such as lean working.

Functional-based working has many disadvantages from a strategic management point of view. Strategic priorities are likely to become fragmented as critical business processes are chopped into disjointed pieces and scattered across several specialized departments. This can result in hand-offs between activities, which lengthen completion time and increase delays and the costs of coordination and overheads. There is a risk that strategy-related essentials fall through departmental cracks or are lost in functional silos. Breaking strategy into specialized pieces is to lose sight of the reasons for strategic imperatives, with the result that employees do not follow through to make sure strategy is being done.

Process organization

A business process is a sequence of tasks to deliver a business objective. Classically, processes are understood as informal cross-functional activities that cross the vertical and hierarchical structure of an organization. The hierarchical structure provides a stable administrative framework, and the processes are the organizing activity within that framework. Following Japanese practice, a new view of business processes came into being – that they should be organized around the pull of customer requirements rather than pushed top down by specialist planners and designers. For business process management the processes decide, bottom up, the things required from the specialists. However, the deployment of a top-level strategy still requires coordination across functional areas.

Cross-functional structure

Companies such as Toyota claim that management of cross-functional objectives across their functional areas is a key strategic resource. This has been compared to making cloth, which involves crossing a horizontal woof (or weft) over a vertical warp to make a strongly held textile (see Figure 9.2): the functional areas of a business are the woof, and centrally organized cross-functional committees act as the warp by carrying out periodic reviews of the management of strategic objectives in the functional areas.

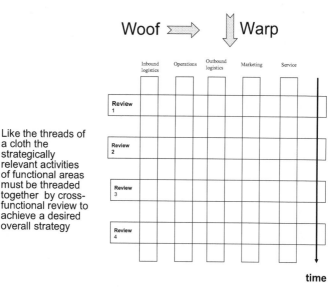

Figure 9.2 Cross-functional woof to weave functional warp

Downsizing

Increasing environmental dynamism and uncertainty brought about by globalization and the emergence of new forms of hyper-competition, such as that from Internet businesses, have made restructuring and downsizing popular. Yale sociologist Richard Sennett (2006) has written about the flexible organization of the new capitalism: cutting-edge firms need people who can learn new skills rather than cling to old competencies. He argues the dynamic organization emphasizes the ability to process and interpret changing bodies of information and practice. A person's worth as a strategist is less their ability based on previous experience and more about how capable they are in dealing with new subjects and problems.

Downsizing is associated with business process re-engineering, which was originally defined as the use of information technology to radically redesign business processes but has come to mean generally the redesign of business processes that results in breakthrough change. The principle is for a senior management team to question how a corporation should be structured for its strategic purpose if it were to be reorganized from scratch. It usually leads to the creation of a flatter organizational structure with less middle management. This can remove a main support for organizing since it diminishes collective corporate memory.

Downsizing is also associated with outsourcing. This is transferring internal activities to an outside organization; typically, these are activities that do not contribute directly to value and can be performed more efficiently outside. Outsourced activities include many support functions, sometimes called back office operations, such as recruitment, accounting, and information technology. It is risky if a breakdown in service affects essential activities because a response cannot easily be controlled from the centre.

Systems and systems thinking

Systems are formal frameworks, documented codes, policies, and procedures which condition routines and normal ways of working. They are important to hierarchical structure because they clarify responsibilities and reporting procedures. System boundaries span large parts of an organization and have interconnected components that work together. A 'systems' way of thinking implies that people will see the whole picture, while in a functionally top-down organization there is always a danger of sub-optimization. A systems approach for strategic management is to take a holistic view of an organization's activities and provide an integrative conceptual framework to guide strategic decisions. The best-known is the McKinsey & Company's 7S framework.

McKinsey's 7S framework

The framework was introduced by Tom Peters and Robert Waterman in their bestselling book *In Search of Excellence* (1982). In looking at an organization as a whole, seven factors are important to driving change, but the

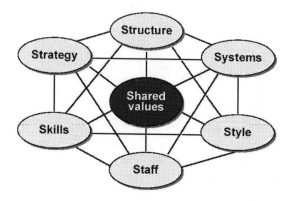

Figure 9.3 Organizing for interconnectivity

essential thing about them is that they are interlinked. No one factor can be treated in isolation; they have to work together (see Figure 9.3).

1   Strategy: those actions an organization plans in response to, or anticipation of, changes in the external environment, its customers, and competitors
2   Structure: the organization that divides tasks and provides for their coordination
3   Systems: the processes, procedures, formal, and informal
4   Style: the perception a senior management team creates of itself in the organization
5   Staff: the socialization of managers in terms of what the business is about
6   Skills: the characterization of the organization in terms of what it does best, its dominating attributes, or capabilities
7   Shared values (or superordinate goals): the guiding beliefs or fundamental ideas around which an organization is built

Making changes in strategy, structure, and systems can be implemented quickly, but to be fully effective the other factors must be strategically managed as well, especially shared values, a concept that is virtually the same as core values (see Chapter 2). Changes in non-strategy and structure factors can take years to achieve; the real pace of change is ultimately a function of all seven variables.

Soft strategy

In the 1980s, about the time of the introduction of the 7S framework, management writers and consultants were stressing the so-called 'softball' nature of competitive advantage in providing an ambiguous organizational culture and attendant interdependences that are hard for rivals to emulate. Some went further and argued for a soft-based approach to running organizations. Sumantra Ghoshal and Christopher Bartlett (1997) argued for the replacement of what they termed hard elements – such as strategy, structure, and systems – with soft ones, namely purpose, which they saw as setting a strategic direction; process, the use of self-directing teams; and people, or the facilitation of commitment and involvement. This implies a lack of formal structure which is likely to make organizing difficult for strategic management.

A related term is strategic architecture, used to refer to networks and infrastructural elements, including a mix of formal and informal management systems and organizational culture, which are coordinated to link up activities and influence behaviour. Architecture is hardwired into an organization in the same way that a building's design will condition how people work. This idea might be consistent with the provision of a strategic dynamic capability to reconfigure and sustain core competencies or strategic assets (see chapter 4).

Karl Weick (1979) introduced a fluid view of strategic organizing when he argued that it is how organizational elements come together frequently and loosely which determines how an organization works as an entity. Using ideas originally associated with biology, Weick argued that means are loosely coupled to an objective, in the sense that they represent alternative pathways. In contrast to classical views of administration that complex systems should be decomposed into stable subassemblies, Weick argued that strategic management should be loosely coupled, involving impermanence, dissolvability, and tacitness. Managing strategic objectives is more like scoring goals in a football game than, say, driving your car to a preprogrammed destination.

Strategic planning – revisited

Where does this leave strategic planning? The days of classical forward strategic planning are gone. Strategic plans have become shorter-term programmes, more goal-focused, and less specific about how activities and resources are worked out at local levels. The role of strategic planning is now less about formal strategic decision-making and more a framework for coordinating how people are managing strategically linked activities in practice. Implementation is carried out through an organization's structure and control systems, but it is generally recognized that strategy forms during its execution during daily management.

Strategic planning is primarily an implementation activity for many large and complex organizations, and it works through medium-term plans. The medium-term business plan is essentially a guiding framework for the detail to be worked out during annual planning at a daily management level. This is the subject of the following chapter.

References

Chandler Jr., A. D. (1962), *Strategy and Structure: Chapters in the History of the Industrial Enterprise*, Cambridge, MA: MIT Press.

Daft, R. (2012), *Understanding the Theory and Design of Organizations*, Andover: Cengage Learning.

Ghoshal, S., & Bartlett, C. (1997), *The Individualised Corporation: Great Companies Are Defined by Purpose, Process and People*, London: William Heinemann.

Peters, T., & Waterman, R. H. (1982), *In Search of Excellence*, London: Harper and Row.

Sennett, R. (2006), *The Culture of the New Capitalism*, London: Yale University Press.

Weick, K. E. (1979), *The Social Psychology of Organizing*, 2nd edit. Reading, MA: Addison-Wesley.

10 Strategic control

Essential summary

Strategic control is the monitoring and review of an organization's strategic management of purpose, objectives, and strategy; this involves organizing and managing adaptations and changes during the on-going execution of strategy.

The role of strategy in operations once it has been implemented has been a neglected area of strategic management.

The *execution of strategy* is the management of strategy during daily management and operations once strategy has been put in place in the organization.

Strategic performance management is a strategically managed system that enables a senior level to execute and manage the delivery of its strategic priorities.

Levers of strategic control are four information-based systems that senior managers can use to lever an organization into a desired strategic position.

Strategic control is top management's overall control of the effectiveness of its strategic management, including its longer- and shorter-term components. This includes the execution of strategy in daily management driven by an organization-wide system of review (Kaplan and Norton, 2008). Strategic review is central to strategic control since it plays a critical role in the strategy learning process and brings an organization's leadership team together to focus on long-term improvement. However, checks and reviews of strategically linked activities run through the whole enterprise, and to be sure that strategic review at the top of the organization is effective, the whole system of organizational multi-level review should itself be reviewed and understood by senior management.

The review wheel

Three factors should be distinguished in understanding an organization's system of review: long-term purpose, objectives, and strategy; shorter-term implementation and execution; and overall feedback on performance in the light of purpose (see Figure 10.1). The shaded boxes at the top left denote longer-term purpose, objectives, and strategy. The shaded boxes at the top right denote implementation and execution (the shorter-term management of strategic performance) (Witcher and Chau, 2014).

A review wheel is positioned bottom left to show several levels of periodic review. At its centre is the daily management of operations, where processes are being continuously monitored, subject to the PDCA principle; periodic review in operations is frequent and single-looped, involving corrective and exploitive learning (see chapter 4). The next level involves less frequent strategic reviews of the progress of strategically linked priorities; these are primarily double-looped and involve explorative learning. The last level on the wheel is an annual diagnostic or business audit of the management of the core areas of the organization.

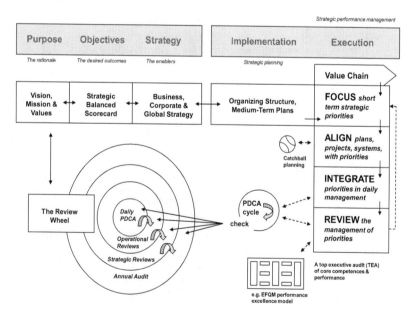

Figure 10.1 A review wheel for strategic management

These levels of review feed into each other to inform a top-level review of long-term purpose, objectives, and strategy so that if necessary, these can be adapted, followed up, and changed. The review of the longer-term components of strategic management should be a shaping, reflective, and testing activity. Strategy's execution – shown in Figure 10.1 to the right as a descending box through focus, alignment, integration, and review – is about strategy in action.

Strategic performance management

Strategic performance management is the translation of longer-term objectives and strategy into daily management. Top management deals with implementation by putting in place organizational structures and systems, but there also needs to be an organizing framework for executing strategy in daily management. Strategic objectives are passed into operational management as medium-term plans, which are developed as annual KPI targets to use in process management.

KPIs are translated as targets to drive incremental and continuous improvement in business processes. At the same time, a small number of visionary strategic objectives are introduced to use as overall strategic priorities. These typically require rethinking how processes are organized and perform. The strategic performance management process is based on an annual sequence of strategic focus, alignment, integration, and review – an annual FAIR cycle (see Figure 10.2) (Witcher and Butterworth, 1999).

The annual sequence follows through first focusing the organization on the strategic objectives. These are then used to strategically align action

Figure 10.2 The annual FAIR cycle for managing strategic objectives

plans and systems used for routine annual planning at operational levels. Daily management is carried out based on these plans so that the strategic objectives are integrated into operations. Finally, towards the end of the cycle, the progress and the management of strategic objectives are reviewed, and the lessons are used to inform the refocusing of the objectives for the next turn of the cycle for the following year.

Focus

The primary participants in the focus phase of the cycle are senior managers, who are part of a team typically composed of departmental and functional heads. The first concern is to establish the operational needs of departments (illustrated in Figure 10.3). The aim here is to ensure that the core areas of the organization are working to maximize value. A second concern is to establish cross-functional needs to ensure that strategic objectives are in balance across departments. These are shown grouped on the left-hand side of the figure as balanced scorecard objectives. KPIs are developed by the senior management team, which addresses both the customized needs of the departments in creating value and the cross-functional needs of the

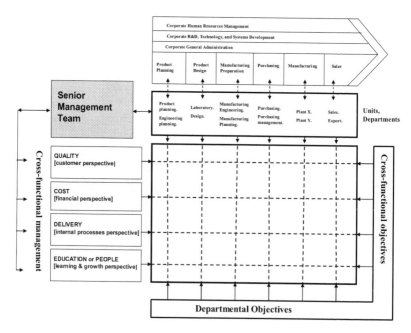

Figure 10.3 The development of annual strategic objectives and KPIs

organization's strategy. The KPIs are used in daily management to drive continuous improvement.

Lastly, the senior management team selects a small number of annual strategic objectives which serve as the overall priorities for bringing about a degree of innovatory change that would not otherwise be accomplished through routine management. Their purpose is to encourage exploratory organizational learning – as they are typically ambitious – and ask an organization to rethink its existing organizational routines.

The content of an annual strategic objective will depend upon two main things: a need to address an issue concerned with the organization's mission and a need to move the organization significantly forward to a new visionary position. The essential thing is that these strategic objectives are annual priorities to be addressed by everyone and thus must be very few in number, say, between one and four: that is, they are regarded as the vital few.

Alignment

The vital few are taken and used at other levels in an organization as their own strategic priorities to include in local routine planning. While planning is primarily centred on local priorities and KPIs, the vital few objectives take priority as a vehicle for coordinating routine plans. This involves crafting draft action plans and passing them between teams to reach agreements with potential participants about how the objectives can be achieved in routine operations (see Figure 10.4).

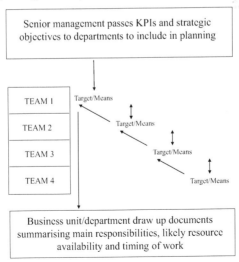

Figure 10.4 Playing catchball in planning

The development of action plans is an iterative activity as affected parties and potential participants are sounded out; the passing of possibilities to and from is like a game of catch, and this activity is called catchball. Typically, subordinate teams have to bring their ideas to superiors and may have to modify their plans, perhaps several times. Both targets and the means to achieve them are considered together for carrying plans out.

Some strategic objectives may need a long development period to sort out their implications for daily management. Typically, these need to clarify the extent of their relevance for a number of activities including departmental collaboration. A problem-solving activity of this kind is usually a task for project management. Once catchball nears completion, departmental management oversees the implications of the agreements to check that the required workload and level of resources are feasible.

Integration

As soon as plans are completed, teams begin to manage their processes with the newly agreed objectives as a part of their daily management routines. Management philosophies and business methodologies come into their own during integration. The organizing principle for the management of objectives is the PDCA cycle (see chapter 4); work is monitored to plan (objectives), and teams intervene to correct deviations through problem-solving and act to make sure changes are effective. A feature of good process management is to be sure that objectives are transparent and relevant. Departmental heads have to ensure that budgets, staff appraisals, and incentives are consistent with the management of plans. It is important to be sure that individuals are not over-loaded and are able to receive the support they need for development.

This is a very different approach from management by objectives (MbO), which is still used widely in organizations. MbO is an approach that deploys strategy and cascades objectives down through the levels of an organization by subdividing them so that a superior's objectives become the subobjectives of subordinates, who in turn pass their objectives across to their own subordinates, and so on. This puts an emphasis on the achievement of objectives rather than the how-to, or the process, of achieving them.

Review

The review phase of the annual FAIR cycle systematically involves the participation of the top executive and senior manager level in an audit of how the core areas of an organization are being managed in relation to strategy and purpose. This activity goes under various names; the most common are 'executive audit' and 'president's diagnosis'. It involves the participation of top and senior levels of management, and the aim is to make a diagnosis about the most important issues through listening to reports and personal accounts given by personnel in different parts of the organization.

It takes place towards the end of the annual FAIR cycle and represents its review phase. The participation of the top level as auditors is important since it provides a basis to understand how the organization's strategy is being executed at operational levels. It also provides intelligence for the next focus phase. The auditing activity puts senior managers in touch with operational realities, and their presence helps to provide leadership and motivation for lower-level management with overall strategy. In this way the activity provides a lever for a form of strategic control that stimulates organizational learning and the emergence of new strategies.

The Nissan Motor Company identifies 13 core business areas for creating value (Witcher, Chau, and Harding, 2008). It also specifies seven core competencies: daily control; the determination of the vital few objectives; the coordination of the vital few through development and deployment; the establishment of control items (targets and means); analytical and problem-solving abilities; check and action taken; and leadership and participation by high-ranking personnel.

Corporate headquarters reviews annually its subsidiary organizations to understand and influence how Nissan managers and employees are using the core competencies in the core business areas. Once completed, a two-page status report is released across the corporate group to compare how the subsidiaries score for the level of development they have reached for each of the competencies. In this way the results are visible. If feedback is managed carefully by the centre, the shortcomings of a strategy will be apparent.

Levers of strategic control

Robert Simons (1995), an accounting specialist at the Harvard Business School, has offered a strategic control framework to understand how senior managers gather information to progress strategy. In doing so he observes that control systems must accommodate not only intended strategies but also those to emerge from local experimentation and independent staff initiatives. He identifies four types of systems: beliefs, boundary, diagnostic control, and interactive control. Senior managers can use these systems to lever an organization into a desired strategic position.

Lever 1: belief systems

Belief systems inspire and direct the search for new opportunities. This is done through an explicit set of purpose statements that senior managers communicate formally and reinforce systematically to provide the basic values and direction for the organization. The notion of belief suggests an organization's values must be deeply rooted and based on the purpose for its existence. Simons did not originally include beliefs but later changed his mind as they reflect a contemporary stress on vision and its importance to leadership.

Lever 2: boundary systems

Boundary systems set the limits to the opportunity-seeking behaviour of belief systems. They consist of sets of rules and sanctions that restrict search, but at the same time they help clarify those areas of risk that the organization ought to avoid. Boundary systems include various organizational constraints, such as specific and stringent codes of conduct. These may be influences on things like regulatory requirements and political and public opinion. The role of senior management is to state and cascade the core values and visions of an organization, analyze business risks, and focus subordinates to ease pressures brought about by scope and scale.

Lever 3: diagnostic control systems

Diagnostic control systems motivate and monitor organizational behaviour towards the achievement of specified goals. These are formal systems designed to monitor the progress of objectives in the implementation and execution of strategic and related plans. They provide a diagnostic check on how strategy is working. They also motivate, monitor, and reward the achievement of specified goals. These are feedback systems that are core to management control. Managers obtain feedback from their subordinates to align the organization's activities with the organizational goals.

Simons outlined three abilities for diagnostic control: to measure the outputs of a process, to predetermine standards against which results are compared, and to be able to correct deviations from these standards. These ensure managers can control outputs through a careful selection of inputs and can deal with those critical performance variables representing important dimensions of a strategy. Diagnostic control systems can be devolved to local management and, unlike boundary systems, individuals have the freedom to accomplish the desired ends as superiors will have already agreed to the process specification. Senior managers will only become involved by exception.

Lever 4: interactive control systems

Interactive control systems stimulate an organization by provoking emergent new ideas; these comprise formal information systems that managers use to involve themselves regularly and personally in the decision activities of subordinates. Many kinds of interactive controls are used, but the important element is the personal participation of senior managers in reviews of progress, especially for cross-functional face-to-face meetings. These enable senior managers to try out and introduce new possibilities for change. This activity helps form the agendas for wider debate and includes information-gathering from outside routine channels.

Simons notes three distinctive characteristics of interactive control systems: information is generated by the system and addressed by senior management; operating managers with other levels of an organization must review the system frequently; and the data generated must be discussed face-to-face in meetings at all levels. This system is a lever and catalyst for all the action plans of an organization.

Simons argues for a balance in control between positive and negative control so that the restricting attributes of boundary and diagnostic systems are harmonious with the more expansive attributes of belief and interactive systems. Strategic performance management puts a stress on diagnostic and interactive control. However, for effective strategic management, there needs to be a consistent focus on the overall key strategic priorities in daily management, with a stress on the 'how to get things done' rather than the 'what to do'. If things are done in the right way, it will be more apparent if the right things are being done. In all of this there still has to be a belief in the importance of information and evidence in addressing issues.

References

Kaplan, R. S., & Norton, D. P. (2008), *The Execution Premium: Linking Strategy to Operations for Competitive Advantage*, Cambridge, MA: Harvard Business Press.

Simons, R. (1995), *Levers of Control: How Managers Use Innovative Control Systems*, Boston, MA: Harvard Business School Press.

Witcher, B. J., & Butterworth, R. (1999), Hoshin kanri: How Xerox manages, *Long Range Planning*, 32, 323–332.

Witcher, B. J., & Chau, V. S. (2014), *Strategic Management: Principles and Practice*, Andover: Cengage Learning.

Witcher, B. J., Chau, V. S., & Harding, P. (2008), Dynamic capabilities: Top executive audits and hoshin kanri at Nissan South Africa, *International Journal of Operations and Production Management*, 28, 540–561.

11 Strategic leadership

Essential summary

Strategic leadership is how top management and other levels of management lead an organization to work towards achieving the organization's purpose.

Since the primary direction of strategic management is a top-down activity, the nature of top management's approach to leading and influencing the rest of the organization is very important.

The four competencies of leadership comprise the competencies of attention, meaning, trust, and self, each of which has to be managed.

Leadership styles are the distinctive manners in which leaders act to influence the strategic management of their organizations.

Leadership and management may have different characteristics; an understanding of their differences is important if they are to work together to promote effective strategic management.

The prime responsibility for strategic management and making sure that it works lies at the top of the organization. The executive and other senior managers must lead the organization so that it will achieve its purpose. Effective strategic leadership is the foundation for successfully using the strategic management process.

Leadership is the ability of an individual or a group of individuals to influence others to achieve an organization's purpose and objectives. Strategic leadership is the style and general approach embodied and used by a senior management to articulate purpose, objectives, and strategy to influence implementation and strategic control through the organization. Its nature varies at different stages of an organization's development, especially with scale when senior levels become more distant from daily management. Leadership styles vary according to the personalities and group dynamics of senior managers. However, whatever the form and style, strategic leadership should work to promote organization-wide synergy and harmony.

The popular notion of a leader is that of a person who is followed by others. There may be any number of reasons for following, but it is usually that leaders exercise a power to influence events. In the context of strategic management a leader is one who by influencing others has an ability to take the organization forward to a common purpose. The most powerful people in an organization in this sense are, of course, the executives and other senior managers; they make the most important strategic decisions. While decisions may emerge and be worked out involving many people, in the end it is only the top managers who make the decisions (or choose not to make them) for an organization as a whole.

At every organizational level there will be people with leadership qualities and abilities: those who lead units, sections, teams and those who are specialists in important areas of knowledge and competency. Many of these, located in different parts of an organization, will be important in influencing and empowering others to create strategic change as necessary. The ability to manage people is central, especially to develop core competencies.

In a book about the learning organization, Peter Senge (2006) argued for a kind of organizational leadership that enhances strategic skills and decision-making. A leader is anybody who is able to carry out three roles: a designer of organizational conditions to enable the sort of people who say 'we did it ourselves'; a teacher who shows people how to self-develop in a way that is a priority for the organization; and a steward who uses strategic purpose to bring a depth of meaning to an individual's aspirations. There is also an extra ability – to use systems thinking to be able to see and understand the important organizational interdependencies that condition action and relations.

Observers, in general, suggest an effective leader should be able to skillfully switch between different leadership styles, depending upon the situation they are being faced with at any one time. To a degree this rests upon a leader's emotional intelligence: an ability to recognize and understand their own emotions and the emotions of others. High emotional intelligence includes an ability to articulate openly about feelings, to control and use emotions to good effect, and to empathize with others. Perhaps this is expecting a lot, but it is important to at least consider these qualities.

Executive leadership is by its nature remote in the sense that only a small part of a large organization's staff will have regular contact with top managers. In this case the appearance of leadership is important. Niccolo Machiavelli (1532), writing about princes in the early sixteenth century, observed that men in general judge by their eyes rather than by their heads. While everyone is in a position to watch, few are in a position to come in close touch with senior managers. Everyone sees what you appear to be; few experience what you really are. What leaders do, as represented in the symbols and artefacts associated with them, is important as an indicator of credibility and legitimacy.

Four competencies of leadership

Warren Bennis and Burt Nanus (1985), identified four management competencies for good leadership – attention, meaning, trust, and self.

The management of attention

This is an ability to attract and draw people to them, to hold their attention and inspire them. It is typically associated with charismatic leadership; although a leader can be ordinary, it is the intensity of an associated vision that inspires and gives a sense of conviction about what should happen next and that it will happen.

The management of meaning

This is a sense of understanding underlying patterns so that apparently unrelated elements can be communicated as a coherent and understandable whole. Despite a messy complexity, followers need to see the way forward to be able to respond with an organized energy and focus. It is not enough to be informed; it is necessary to use language and visual slogans that communicate clarity. Explanations should be kept simple and abstract in a straightforward way.

The management of trust

A leader needs to be trusted to keep to a constant theme; in other words, although an organization must periodically change objectives as events unfold, a leader must be true to his or her underlying principles. These may not be articulated as such, but a sense of who the leader is and what they stand for should hold and be conveyed in similar phrases and slogans, repeated over. A constancy of purpose must be felt by others if loyalty is to be maintained over time, or else they will feel betrayed.

The management of self

A leader should know his or her abilities and thus not worry about taking decisions or agonizing over progress and results. He or she will reflect just long enough on mistakes to learn from experience and will move ahead again quickly. This gives confidence to others; it is not the confidence of leaders as such but the sureness of their bearing and actions that counts.

Leadership styles

James McGregor Burns (1978), a political scientist, in his book *Leadership*, distinguishes between transformational and transactional leadership. Transformational leadership is inspirational in a way that exploits the motives and higher needs of the follower, so the 'full person of the follower is engaged'. He suggests that the relations between most leaders and followers are transactional, when leaders approach followers to exchange one thing for another; bargaining is central to most of the relationships between leaders and followers. These ideas have been influential for strategy programmes (see Figure 11.1).

Transformational leadership associates individual self-interest with the larger vision of an organization to inspire a sense of collective vision. When effective, it creates excitement and raises enthusiasm for the challenges to

Transformational leadership	Leaders have a clear view of purpose as a desired future state. They are more concerned with objectives that indicate a broad direction rather than its detail, which is left to others to determine.
Transactional leadership	Leaders have a view of purpose as mission. They are more concerned with objectives linked to a clear programme of change that ensures staff know what is expected of them.
Charismatic or visionary leadership	Leaders embody a strong (often personalised brand) image that is distinctive. They scan opportunities in the external environment and sense purpose, sometimes as entrepreneurial action.
Quiet, participative leadership	Leaders involve others in understanding purpose as core values to share common ways of working (core competences) and participate in setting objectives so that they are more committed to executing them.

Figure 11.1 Leadership styles

bring about change. Transactional leadership, on the other hand, is more centred on mission and those explicit management systems used to clarify expectations and agreements and provide constructive feedback about performance.

A heightened form of transformational leadership is characterized by a charismatic dominant personality, which is a useful quality to force things past obstacles, but the kind of dramatic success that charismatic leadership achieves can lead to hubris and a style of leadership that wants to micro manage. This is abrasive if subordinates think a chief executive should be a thoughtful listener and a participant in collegial styles of leadership. A contrasting style of leadership is low key, often self-effacing, and quiet.

Great companies, according to Jim Collins, have leaders who do not force change or try to directly motivate people; rather, they have leaders who work with an organization's core values. Leaders work to build up a disciplined organizational culture that sustains results over the long term. This is not command and control, but it does require everybody to adhere to a consistent working system and is about giving people the freedom to engage in disciplined thought and then follow it with artful action. Collins claims that problems of commitment, alignment, motivation, and change melt away as they take care of themselves with a clear, disciplined way of working.

Leadership and management

A distinction is often drawn between leadership and strategy on the one side and management and control on the other. This is a view that encourages senior managers to think that they do strategy, while others do management. This separation originally began with the classical notion that strategy implementation should follow formulation (see chapter 1). The view that leadership is different from management is strongly felt.

Abraham Zaleznik (1977), writing in the *Harvard Business Review* was one of the first to argue that leadership and management are different roles: a leader is a change shaper and mover, while a manager is focused on processes, teamwork, and working within the existing organization. In some national cultures the difference is not readily understood; in Japan, for instance, there is no equivalent separation – leaders expect to manage.

Warren Bennis (1993) has listed the differences between management and leadership activities (see Figure 11.2). While leading is about influencing people to go in a certain direction, managing is about having responsibility to accomplish the action.

Unfortunately, the two sides do not often talk to each other. Strategic management requires leadership to understand how its organization manages purpose, especially in those core business areas or processes that are vital

Leaders	Managers
• Innovate	• Administers
• Develops	• Maintains
• Investigates	• Accepts reality
• Focuses on people	• Systems and structures
• Inspires trust	• Relies on control
• Long-range perspective	• Short-range
• Asks what and why	• Asks how and when
• Eye on the horizon	• Bottom-line
• Originates	• Imitates
• Challenges status quo	• Accepts status quo
• His/her own person	• Classic good soldier

Figure 11.2 The different characteristics of leadership and management

to competitive advantage. In this, domain knowledge is important; this is knowledge and experience of how an organization works. This is a difficult area for leaders who are brought in from outside an organization. This is especially so for strategic management if competitive advantage rests on firm-specific strategic resources.

Strategic change

An organizational culture starts with the leadership provided by an organization's founder. The core values laid down in the early days and the evolution and growth of an organization subsequently imprints a distinctiveness that is likely to last long after the departure of the original founders and managers. As an organization grows, it attracts new members who are inspired by and share the original values. An organization's culture becomes more distinct as its membership grows more similar. However, group-think is a disadvantage if events call for radical change.

When the need comes, perhaps because of a crisis, it is difficult for a new leader and team to carry out a change programme. John Kotter (1996), professor of leadership at Harvard, devised a sequence of eight stages for leading strategic and cultural change. He argues they are all necessary and any failure to carry them is the reason for failure in change programmes:

1   Establish a sense of urgency: this makes others aware of the need for change and works to action them quickly while motivation is strong.
2   Create a guiding coalition: put together a group that has enough power to drive the change and can work as a team.

3   Develop a change vision: change direction to develop strategies for achieving the vision.

4   Communicate a vision for others to buy into: as many as possible need to understand and accept the vision with its associated strategies – a vision should be communicated by a factor of 10, 100, even 1,000.

5   Empower action across the organization: remove obstacles to change; change systems and structures that seriously undermine the vision; encourage risk-taking and non-traditional ideas, activities, and actions.

6   Generate short-term wins: plan for achievements that can easily be made visible and follow through with these to recognize and reward those employees who were involved.

7   Never let up: continuously sustain and reinforce the increasing credibility of the change and recruit, promote champions, develop these and other employees who can implement the vision; reinvigorate the change process with new projects, themes, and change agents.

8   Incorporate changes into the culture: the new ways of doing things must be seen to compare favourably with traditional ways; articulate the connections between the new behaviours and organizational success; develop the means to ensure leadership development and succession.

Kotter's sequence for change is sensible, but perhaps perseverance is the most important leadership principle for change (and luck). However, it is to be remembered that most organizations are everyday affairs and the people in them (including customers) are human beings. Organizations and people are rarely perfect for strategic management. So it is absolutely essential for leaders to be both tough-skinned and open-minded. They have to lead and manage their organizations no matter what the circumstances, and, in the end, it is not strategy but how strategy is managed that really counts.

For strategic management to be effective, leaders need to be able to see and understand the big picture of the organization in terms of purpose – its external and internal environment. Different and often contrasting and conflicting strands of information must be considered against a broad array of possibilities and outcomes. Objectives should be both certain and yet pragmatic. The approaches or strategy used to progress strategic objectives should over time be sustainable and clear about competitive advantage. Organizational structure and strategic planning should be conducive and lead to an effective execution of strategy in daily management. Leaders need to understand their organizations and adopt an appropriate style fit for carrying out the long-term purpose.

References

Bennis, W. (1993), *An Invented Life: Reflections on Leadership and Change*, Reading, MA: Addison-Wesley.

Bennis W. & Nanus B. (1985), *Leaders: The Strategies for Taking Charge*, New York: Harper & Row.

Burns, J. M. (1978), *Leadership*, New York: Harper & Row.

Kotter, J. P. (1996), *Leading Change*, Boston: Harvard Business School Press.

Machiavelli, N. (1535), available as Machiavelli, Niccolò (1985), *The Prince*, University of Chicago Press. Translated by Harvey Mansfield.

Senge, P. (2006), *The Fifth Discipline: The Art and Practice of the Learning Organization*, New York: Doubleday.

Zaleznik, A. (1977), Managers and leaders: Are they different? *Harvard Business Review*, 55(5).

Index

Printed in the United States
by Baker & Taylor Publisher Services